GOOD EATING

ONE-POT MEALS

GOOD EATING

ONE-POT MEALS

YOUR COMPLETE GUIDE TO PERFECT ONE-POT MEALS EVERY TIME

This edition published in 2012

LOVE FOOD is an imprint of Parragon Books Ltd

Parragon
Queen Street House
4 Queen Street
Bath BA1 1HE, UK

Copyright © Parragon Books Ltd 2008

LOVE FOOD and the accompanying heart device is a registered trademark of Parragon Books Ltd in
Australia, the UK, USA, India, and the EU.

www.parragon.com

ISBN 978-1-4454-6611-8

Printed in China

Cover design by Talking Design
Photography by Mike Cooper
Food styling by Sumi Glass and Lincoln Jefferson
Introduction by Christine McFadden

This book uses both imperial and metric measurements. Follow the same units of measurement
throughout; do not mix imperial and metric. All spoon measurements are level: teaspoons are assumed to
be 5 ml, and tablespoons are assumed to be 15 ml. Unless otherwise stated, milk is assumed to be whole,
eggs and individual vegetables are medium, and pepper is freshly ground black pepper.

The times given are an approximate guide only. Preparation times differ according to the techniques used
by different people and the cooking times may also vary from those given as a result of the type of oven
used. Optional ingredients, variations, or serving suggestions have not been included in the calculations.

Recipes using raw or very lightly cooked eggs should be avoided by infants, the elderly, pregnant women,
convalescents, and anyone with a chronic condition. Pregnant and breast-feeding women are advised to
avoid eating peanuts and peanut products. People with nut allergies should be aware that some of the
prepared ingredients used in the recipes in this book may contain nuts. Always check the package before
use.

CONTENTS

INTRODUCTION

These days most of us lead action-packed lives, either at work or as a busy parent, or both. Time-consuming meal preparation, let alone clearing up afterwards, just doesn't fit in very easily. Yet most of us care about health and want to eat nutritious home-cooked food. What could be more satisfying than something simmering on the stove, filling the air with delicious aromas?

If you love cooking but are short of time, then *The Big Book of One Pot* will be a lifesaver. As the name suggests, all the dishes can be cooked in a single pot with other ingredients, leaving you with very little to wash up but plenty of time to get on with other things.

The one pot method is a relaxed and flexible way of cooking, easily adjusted to whatever ingredients you have in your fridge or store cupboard. If one ingredient is missing, it's usually possible to substitute another. If you're short of space or equipment, one pot cooking is ideal – you need just one pot and a single burner.

One pot cooking doesn't limit you to soups and stews, though the book contains plenty of recipes for these. In many parts of the world, cooking in a single pot is the norm, whether it's a cauldron, a wok, a tagine or a bean pot. Many dishes grew up out of necessity when food and fuel were scarce. Others were created for religious reasons – the Muslim Ramadan, for example, or the Jewish Sabbath when orthodox believers are forbidden to work or cook. The pot could be left to simmer slowly overnight, ready to serve at sunset the following day. In cold climates, it was the conviviality and friendship of communal eating that inspired many one pot dishes. Think of Swiss fondue, Hungarian goulash or Mongolian hot pot.

As the recipes in the book demonstrate, this no-frills way of cooking is the ultimate in convenience since everything is ready at the same time. It's the ideal food for solitary suppers or for feeding a crowd. Just put the pot on the table and tuck in.

GETTING STARTED

Although one pot cooking appears simple, it relies on a certain amount of pre-planning to ensure that things go smoothly. More importantly, getting organised from the start means you can relax and enjoy the actual process of cooking instead of running round the kitchen looking for missing utensils or, worse still, discovering too late that you've run out of a vital ingredient.

Before you start to cook:

- Read the recipe all the way through, then plan the sequence according to what needs soaking, chopping, precooking etc.
- Have the right tools and cookware to hand
- Make sure knives are sharp
- Wash fresh vegetables, fruits and herbs
- Assemble all the ingredients then measure or weigh them as necessary
- Complete any pre-preparation such as chopping or grating
- Have the prepared ingredients lined up in bowls, ready to add to the pot at the correct time
- Clear up as you go along

USEFUL UTENSILS

As well as basics such as knives and chopping boards, there are a number of additional utensils that make one pot cooking easier and safer.

Though you can happily leave the pot to simmer while you get on with something else, it's still important to keep track of temperature and time. Thermometers are essential for food safety, and a timer with a loud ring is invaluable for reminding you when the dish needs your attention. You'll also need spoons and spatulas for stirring, and tools for turning and lifting ingredients that are precooked in stages before they go into the pot. A sturdy long-handled fork or multi-pronged meat lifter are handy for large pieces of meat, while stainless steel spring-action tongs allow you to clasp smaller pieces of food securely. A perforated shallow skimmer is useful for removing froth and scum from the surface of stews.

Although one pot recipes are infinitely flexible, it's worth investing in proper measuring spoons and jugs, as well as kitchen scales, especially if you are new to cooking. Once you gain experience and confidence, it's fine to add a pinch of this and a handful of that.

The joy of one pot meals is that they can be brought straight from oven to table. However, heat can damage unprotected surfaces, so it's a good idea to have a trivet or pot stand at the ready.

COOKWARE

For most of the recipes in this book, a few heavy-based saucepans and casseroles in varying sizes with tight-fitting lids make up the basic equipment. You'll also need a high-sided frying pan, a wok, good-quality roasting tins that won't warp or twist, and some shallow baking dishes for gratins and crumbles.

FRESH PRODUCE

Wholesome fresh vegetables, meat, poultry and fish add valuable nutrients to one pot meals, as well as colour, texture and appetizing flavours.

Vegetables

One of the most important source of vitamins, minerals and fibre, vegetables are packed with carotenoids (the plant form of vitamin A), vitamin C and vitamin E, which collectively protect against heart disease and some cancers.

Meat and poultry

Meat and poultry provide high quality protein, important minerals such as iron and zinc, and B vitamins, needed to release energy from food. Meat tends to be high in fat, so if you're trying to cut down, trim off any excess or choose lean cuts.

Fish and seafood

Dense-fleshed fish and seafood make marvellous one pot meals. They provide protein and essential minerals, while oily fish such as tuna are a unique source of omega-3 fatty acids that protect against heart disease and feed the brain.

Fresh herbs

A generous sprinkling of fresh herbs added at the end of cooking will provide delightful fragrance and colour to one pot meals.

STORE CUPBOARD ITEMS

A store cupboard judiciously stocked with a few essentials means you are never without the makings of a one pot meal.

Grains

Grains such as rice, barley, oats, quinoa and bulgar wheat contain a package of concentrated nutrients. Perked up with colourful spices and herbs, they form a nutritious base to which meat, fish and vegetables can be added as necessary.

Pulses

Dried pulses are packed with nutrients, and provide a mellow background to more strongly flavoured ingredients. Canned pulses are invaluable since you can add them to the pot without soaking or precooking.

Pasta

Short pasta shapes, from tiny star-shapes to coils and fat tubes, make the basis for endless one pot meals. Pasta shapes can be precooked or added to the pot with plenty of liquid.

Seeds and nuts

Crunchy seeds and nuts provide texture and, if chopped finely, can give body to the cooking liquid. Pumpkin, sunflower and sesame seeds are particularly nutritious, as are walnuts, almonds and Brazil nuts.

Sauces and pastes

A judicious splash of sauce or dollop of paste can perk up an otherwise bland dish. Soy sauce, Worcestershire sauce and Tabasco all have outstanding flavours, as do tomato purée, olive paste and mustards. Ready-made jars of ethnic sauces also add exciting flavours, and save time too.

Spices and dried herbs

For the best flavour, buy spices whole (including pepper), and grind them as needed. Rosemary, thyme and oregano are the best herbs to use dried; the more delicate varieties are better when fresh. Add spices and dried herbs at the early stages of cooking to bring out the full flavour.

MAKING THE MOST OF THE POT

One pot meals can be cooked in a variety of pots and pans. Knowing how to get the best from them is invaluable when tackling new recipes.

Casserole

A casserole is ideal for leisurely stews and braises cooked either on the hob or in the oven, and for pot-roasting boned and rolled joints of meat. Poultry thighs and drumsticks and dense-fleshed root vegetables are good too. The moist heat encourages a magical exchange of flavours between meat, vegetables and seasonings, resulting in truly succulent dishes.

After an hour or two with the lid on, test by prodding with a skewer. Meat should feel meltingly tender and root vegetables should be soft but not disintegrating.

High-sided frying-pan

With a tight-fitting lid and heavy ground base, a high-sided pan is perfect for slow-cooked rice dishes such as paella or jambalaya, and for braising larger items like chicken quarters or chops. The generous surface area provides maximum contact with heat, allowing meat to brown quickly before adding other ingredients. The contents can then be covered and left to cook at a leisurely pace.

Wok

Because of the wok's conical shape and continuous stirring, the food continually falls back to the centre where the heat is at its most intense. Since the ingredients are constantly on the move, much less fat is needed, making this a healthy way of cooking.

It is very important to preheat the wok. You should be able to feel the heat radiating from it when you hold your hand flat above the base of the interior. Add the oil only when the wok is really hot.

It is essential to have all the ingredients prepared, ready to add to the wok the minute the oil is at the right heat. It should be almost, but not quite, smoking.

Roasting tin

A good solid roasting tin is ideal for a joint of meat or poultry cooked alongside vegetables such as onions, potatoes, and parsnips. Orange-fleshed vegetables are particularly delicious – try carrots, pumpkin and sweet potato. Make sure the vegetables are cut into similar-sized pieces so that they cook evenly. Tuck some under the meat for extra flavour. A little stock, wine or water is all that's needed to keep everything moist.

Some roasting tins are self-basting. They have dimpled lids that encourage moisture to gather and drip evenly over the contents below, resulting in a particularly succulent dish.

A tin that is sturdy enough to use on the hob means you can speed up the cooking by giving the meat a quick sizzle before it goes into the oven. The caramelised sediment will dissolve and flavour the other ingredients once they give up their liquid.

Baking and gratin dishes

These dishes are for food that is baked in the oven with a browned topping of potato, bubbling cheese, or crunchy breadcrumbs – or all three.

Baking dishes are particularly suitable for one pot meals as they can be brought straight from oven to table, saving on the washing up. They are usually made in attractive shapes and colours.

TOP TIPS FOR PERFECT RESULTS

Once you have tried out a few recipes, you may want to create your own one pot favourites. It's a good idea to follow a few basic techniques:

- Browning meat and poultry before adding other ingredients will produce an appetizing caramelized crust that will dissolve and add flavour to the rest of the dish.

- Add ingredients in descending order of cooking times, slow-cooking dense items first and quick-cooking items last. That way, your one pot meal will have an appetizing texture.

- Add green vegetables just in time to cook them. They'll keep their bright colour and the flavour won't dominate the rest of the dish.

- Best of all is home-made stock, either fresh or frozen. Otherwise use Swiss vegetable bouillon powder – stock cubes can be very salty.

Beef Stock

Makes 1.7 litres/3 pints

Ingredients

1 kg/2 lb 4 oz beef marrow bones, sawn into
7.5-cm/3-inch pieces
650 g/1 lb 7 oz stewing beef in a single piece
2.8 litres/5 pints water
4 cloves
2 onions, halved
2 celery sticks, roughly chopped
8 peppercorns
1 bouquet garni

1 Put the bones in a large, heavy-based
   saucepan and put the stewing beef on top.
   Pour in the water and bring to the boil over
   a low heat. Skim off the scum that rises to
   the surface.

2 Press a clove into each onion half and add
   to the pan with the celery, peppercorns and
   bouquet garni. Partially cover and simmer
   gently for 3 hours. Remove the stewing beef
   from the pan, partially re-cover and simmer
   for a further hour.

3 Remove the pan from the heat and leave to
   cool. Strain the stock into a bowl, cover with
   clingfilm and chill in the refrigerator for at
   least 1 hour and preferably overnight.

4 Remove and discard the layer of fat that has
   set on the surface. Use immediately or freeze
   for up to 6 months.

Chicken Stock

Makes 2.5 litres/4½ pints

Ingredients

1.3 kg/3 lb chicken wings and necks
2 onions, cut into wedges
4 litres/7 pints water
2 carrots, roughly chopped
2 celery sticks, roughly chopped
10 fresh parsley sprigs
4 fresh thyme sprigs
2 bay leaves
10 black peppercorns

1 Place the chicken and onions in a large,
   heavy-based saucepan and cook over a low
   heat, stirring frequently, until browned all over.

2 Pour in the water and stir well, scraping up
   any sediment from the base of the pan. Bring
   to the boil and skim off the scum that rises to
   the surface.

3 Add the carrots, celery, parsley, thyme, bay
   leaves and peppercorns, partially cover the
   pan and simmer gently, stirring occasionally,
   for 3 hours.

4 Remove the pan from the heat and leave to
   cool. Strain the stock into a bowl, cover with
   clingfilm and chill in the refrigerator for at
   least 1 hour and preferably overnight.

5 Remove and discard the layer of fat that has
   set on the surface. Use immediately or freeze
   for up to 6 months.

Fish Stock

Makes 1.3 litres/2¼ pints

Ingredients
650 g/1 lb 7 oz white fish heads, bones
   and trimmings
1 onion, sliced
2 celery sticks, chopped
1 carrot, sliced
1 bay leaf
4 fresh parsley sprigs
4 black peppercorns
¹/₂ lemon, sliced
125 ml/4 fl oz dry white wine
1.3 litres/2¼ pints water

1 Cut out and discard the gills from the fish
heads, then rinse the heads, bones and
trimmings. Place them in a large, heavy-
based saucepan.

2 Add all the remaining ingredients. Bring to the
boil and skim off the scum that rises to the
surface. Lower the heat, partially cover and
simmer gently for 25 minutes.

3 Remove the pan from the heat and leave to
cool. Strain the stock into a bowl, without
pressing down on the contents of the colander.
Use immediately or freeze for up to 3 months.

Vegetable Stock

Makes 2 litres/3¹/₂ pints

Ingredients
2 tbsp sunflower or corn oil
115 g/4 oz onions, finely chopped
115 g/4 oz leeks, finely chopped
115 g/4 oz carrots, finely chopped
4 celery sticks, finely chopped
85 g/3 oz fennel, finely chopped
85 g/3 oz tomatoes, finely chopped
2.25 litres/4 pints water
1 bouquet garni

1 Heat the oil in a large, heavy-based saucepan.
Add the onions and leeks and cook over a low
heat, stirring occasionally, for 5 minutes, until
softened.

2 Add the carrots, celery, fennel and tomatoes,
cover and cook, stirring occasionally, for
10 minutes. Pour in the water, add the
bouquet garni and bring to the boil. Lower
the heat and simmer for 20 minutes.

3 Remove the pan from the heat and leave to
cool. Strain the stock into a bowl. Use
immediately or freeze for up to 3 months.

SOUPS

CHUNKY VEGETABLE SOUP

Put the carrots, onion, garlic, potatoes, celery, mushrooms, tomatoes and stock into a large saucepan. Stir in the bay leaf and herbs. Bring to the boil, then reduce the heat, cover and simmer for 25 minutes.

Add the sweetcorn and cabbage and return to the boil. Reduce the heat, cover and simmer for 5 minutes, or until the vegetables are tender. Remove and discard the bay leaf. Season to taste with pepper.

Ladle into warmed bowls and serve at once with crusty bread rolls.

SERVES 6

2 carrots, sliced

1 onion, diced

1 garlic clove, crushed

350 g/12 oz new potatoes, diced

2 celery sticks, sliced

115 g/4 oz closed-cup mushrooms, quartered

400 g/14 oz canned chopped tomatoes in tomato juice

600 ml/1 pint vegetable stock

1 bay leaf

1 tsp dried mixed herbs or 1 tbsp chopped fresh mixed herbs

85 g/3 oz sweetcorn kernels, frozen or canned, drained

55 g/2 oz green cabbage, shredded

pepper

crusty wholemeal or white bread rolls, to serve

MINESTRONE

Heat the oil in a large saucepan. Add the garlic, onions and Parma ham and cook over a medium heat, stirring, for 3 minutes, until slightly softened. Add the red and orange peppers and the chopped tomatoes and cook for a further 2 minutes, stirring. Stir in the stock, then add the celery. Drain and add the borlotti beans along with the cabbage, peas and parsley. Season with salt and pepper. Bring to the boil, then lower the heat and simmer for 30 minutes.

Add the vermicelli to the pan. Cook for a further 10–12 minutes, or according to the instructions on the packet. Remove from the heat and ladle into serving bowls. Garnish with freshly grated Parmesan and serve with fresh crusty bread.

SERVES 4

2 tbsp olive oil

2 garlic cloves, chopped

2 red onions, chopped

75 g/2¾ oz Parma ham, sliced

1 red pepper, deseeded and chopped

1 orange pepper, deseeded and chopped

400 g/14 oz canned chopped tomatoes

1 litre/1¾ pints vegetable stock

1 celery stick, trimmed and sliced

400 g/14 oz canned borlotti beans

100 g/3½ oz green leafy cabbage, shredded

75 g/2¾ oz frozen peas, defrosted

1 tbsp chopped fresh parsley

75 g/2¾ oz dried vermicelli

salt and pepper

freshly grated Parmesan cheese, to garnish

fresh crusty bread, to serve

FRENCH ONION SOUP

SERVES 6

675 g/1 lb 8 oz onions

3 tbsp olive oil

4 garlic cloves, 3 chopped and
  1 peeled but kept whole

1 tsp sugar

2 tsp chopped fresh thyme

2 tbsp plain flour

125 ml/4 fl oz dry white wine

2 litres/3½ pints vegetable stock

6 slices of French bread

300 g/10½ oz Gruyère
  cheese, grated

fresh thyme sprigs, to garnish

Thinly slice the onions. Heat the olive oil in a large, heavy-based saucepan, then add the onions and cook, stirring occasionally, for 10 minutes, until they are just beginning to brown. Stir in the chopped garlic, sugar and thyme, then reduce the heat and cook, stirring occasionally, for 30 minutes, or until the onions are golden brown.

Sprinkle in the flour and cook, stirring for 1–2 minutes. Stir in the wine. Gradually stir in the stock and bring to the boil, skimming off any scum that rises to the surface, then reduce the heat and simmer for 45 minutes. Meanwhile, preheat the grill to medium. Toast the bread on both sides under the grill. Rub the toast with the garlic clove.

Ladle the soup into 6 flameproof bowls set on a baking tray. Float a piece of toast in each bowl and divide the grated cheese among them. Place under the preheated grill for 2–3 minutes, or until the cheese has just melted. Garnish with thyme and serve.

ROASTED VEGETABLE SOUP

Preheat the oven to 190°C/375°F/Gas Mark 5.

Brush a large shallow baking dish with olive oil. Laying them cut-side down, arrange the tomatoes, peppers, courgettes and aubergine in one layer (use two dishes, if necessary). Tuck the garlic cloves and onion pieces into the gaps and drizzle the vegetables with the remaining olive oil. Season lightly with salt and pepper and sprinkle with the thyme.

Place in the preheated oven and bake, uncovered, for 30–35 minutes, or until soft and browned around the edges. Leave to cool, then scrape out the aubergine flesh and remove the skin from the peppers.

Working in batches, put the aubergine and pepper flesh, together with the tomatoes, courgettes, garlic and onion, into a food processor and chop to the consistency of salsa or pickle; do not purée. Alternatively, place in a bowl and chop together with a knife.

Combine the stock and chopped vegetable mixture in a saucepan and simmer over a medium heat for 20–30 minutes, until all the vegetables are tender and the flavours have completely blended.

Stir in the cream and simmer over a low heat for about 5 minutes, stirring occasionally until hot. Taste and adjust the seasoning, if necessary. Ladle the soup into warmed bowls, garnish with basil and serve.

SERVES 6

3 tbsp olive oil

700 g/1 lb 9 oz ripe tomatoes, skinned, cored and halved

3 large yellow peppers, deseeded and halved

3 courgettes, halved lengthways

1 small aubergine, halved lengthways

4 garlic cloves, halved

2 onions, cut into eighths

pinch of dried thyme

1 litre/1¾ pints chicken, vegetable or meat stock

125 ml/4 fl oz single cream

salt and pepper

shredded basil leaves, to garnish

SQUASH, SWEET POTATO & GARLIC SOUP

Preheat the oven to 190°C/375°F/Gas Mark 5.

Cut the sweet potato, squash and shallots in half lengthways, through to the stem end. Scoop the seeds out of the squash. Brush the cut sides with the oil.

Put the vegetables, cut-side down, in a shallow roasting tin. Add the garlic cloves. Roast in the preheated oven for about 40 minutes, until tender and light brown. Set aside to cool.

When cool, scoop the flesh from the sweet potato and squash halves and put in a saucepan with the shallots. Remove the garlic peel and add the soft insides to the other vegetables.

Add the stock and a pinch of salt. Bring just to the boil, reduce the heat and simmer, partially covered, for about 30 minutes, stirring occasionally, until the vegetables are very tender.

Allow the soup to cool slightly, then transfer to a food processor or blender and process until smooth, working in batches, if necessary. (If using a food processor, strain off the cooking liquid and reserve. Process the soup solids with enough cooking liquid to moisten them, then combine with the remaining liquid.)

Return the soup to the rinsed-out saucepan and stir in the cream. Season to taste with salt and pepper, then simmer for 5–10 minutes until completely heated through. Ladle into warmed serving bowls, garnish with pepper and snipped chives and serve.

SERVES 6–8

1 sweet potato, about 350 g/12 oz

1 acorn squash

4 shallots

2 tbsp olive oil

5–6 garlic cloves, unpeeled

850 ml/1½ pints chicken stock

125 ml/4 fl oz single cream

salt and pepper

snipped chives, to garnish

VICHYSSOISE

SERVES 6

3 large leeks

40 g/1½ oz butter

1 onion, thinly sliced

500 g/1 lb 2 oz potatoes, chopped

850 ml/1½ pints vegetable stock

2 tsp lemon juice

pinch of ground nutmeg

¼ tsp ground coriander

1 bay leaf

1 egg yolk

150 ml/5 fl oz single cream

salt and pepper

freshly snipped chives, to garnish

Trim the leeks, removing most of the green part. Slice the white part of the leeks very finely.

Melt the butter in a saucepan. Add the leeks and onion and fry, stirring occasionally, for about 5 minutes without browning.

Add the potatoes, stock, lemon juice, nutmeg, coriander and bay leaf to the pan, season to taste with salt and pepper and bring to the boil. Cover and simmer for about 30 minutes, until all the vegetables are very soft.

Cool the soup a little, remove and discard the bay leaf and then press through a strainer or process in a food processor or blender until smooth. Pour into a clean pan.

Blend the egg yolk into the cream, add a little of the soup to the mixture and then whisk it all back into the soup and reheat gently, without boiling. Adjust the seasoning to taste. Cool and then chill thoroughly in the refrigerator.

Serve the soup sprinkled with freshly snipped chives.

BEEF GOULASH SOUP

Heat the oil in a large wide saucepan over a medium–high heat. Add the beef and sprinkle with salt and pepper. Fry until lightly browned.

Reduce the heat and add the onions and garlic. Cook for about 3 minutes, stirring frequently, until the onions are softened. Stir in the flour and continue cooking for 1 minute.

Add the water and stir to combine well, scraping the bottom of the pan to mix in the flour. Stir in the tomatoes, carrot, pepper, paprika, caraway seeds, oregano and stock.

Bring just to the boil. Reduce the heat, cover and simmer gently for about 40 minutes, stirring occasionally, until all the vegetables are tender.

Add the tagliatelle to the soup and simmer for a further 20 minutes, or until the tagliatelle is cooked.

Taste the soup and adjust the seasoning, if necessary. Ladle into warmed bowls and top each with a tablespoonful of soured cream. Garnish with coriander and serve.

SERVES 6

1 tbsp olive oil

500 g/1 lb 2 oz fresh lean beef mince

2 onions, finely chopped

2 garlic cloves, finely chopped

2 tbsp plain flour

225 ml/8 fl oz water

400 g/14 oz canned chopped tomatoes

1 carrot, finely chopped

225 g/8 oz red pepper, roasted, peeled, deseeded and chopped

1 tsp Hungarian paprika

¼ tsp caraway seeds

pinch of dried oregano

1 litre/1¾ pints beef stock

55 g/2 oz tagliatelle, broken into small pieces

salt and pepper

soured cream and sprigs of fresh coriander, to garnish

BEEF &
BEAN SOUP

Heat the oil in a large saucepan over a medium heat. Add the onion and garlic and cook, stirring frequently, for 3 minutes, or until softened. Add the pepper and carrots and cook for a further 5 minutes.

Meanwhile, drain the beans, reserving the liquid from the can. Place two thirds of the beans, reserving the remainder, in a food processor or blender with the bean liquid and process until smooth.

Add the beef to the saucepan and cook, stirring constantly, to break up any lumps, until well browned. Add the spices and cook, stirring, for 2 minutes. Add the cabbage, tomatoes, stock and puréed beans and season to taste with salt and pepper. Bring to the boil, then reduce the heat, cover and simmer for 15 minutes, or until the vegetables are tender.

Stir in the reserved beans, cover and simmer for a further 5 minutes. Ladle the soup into warmed soup bowls and serve.

SERVES 4

2 tbsp vegetable oil

1 large onion, finely chopped

2 garlic cloves, finely chopped

1 green pepper, deseeded
  and sliced

2 carrots, sliced

400 g/14 oz canned
  black-eyed beans

225 g/8 oz fresh beef mince

1 tsp each ground cumin, chilli
  powder and paprika

¼ cabbage, sliced

225 g/8 oz tomatoes, peeled
  and chopped

600 ml/1 pint beef stock

salt and pepper

CHORIZO & RED KIDNEY BEAN SOUP

SERVES 4

2 tbsp olive oil

2 garlic cloves, chopped

2 red onions, chopped

1 red pepper, deseeded and chopped

2 tbsp cornflour

1 litre/1¾ pints vegetable stock

450 g/1 lb potatoes, peeled, halved and sliced

150 g/5½ oz chorizo, sliced

2 courgettes, trimmed and sliced

200 g/7 oz canned red kidney beans, drained

125 ml/4 fl oz double cream

salt and pepper

thick slices of fresh bread, to serve

Heat the oil in a large saucepan. Add the garlic and onions and cook over a medium heat, stirring, for 3 minutes, until slightly softened. Add the red pepper and cook for a further 3 minutes, stirring. In a bowl, mix the cornflour with enough stock to make a smooth paste and stir it into the pan. Cook, stirring, for 2 minutes. Stir in the remaining stock, then add the potatoes and season with salt and pepper. Bring to the boil, then lower the heat and simmer for 25 minutes, until the vegetables are tender.

Add the chorizo, courgettes and kidney beans to the pan. Cook for 10 minutes, then stir in the cream and cook for a further 5 minutes. Remove from the heat and ladle into serving bowls. Serve with slices of fresh bread.

SOUPS

33

BACON & LENTIL SOUP

Heat a large, heavy-based saucepan or flameproof casserole. Add the bacon and cook over a medium heat, stirring, for 4–5 minutes, or until the fat runs. Add the chopped onion, carrots, celery, turnip and potato and cook, stirring frequently, for 5 minutes.

Add the lentils and bouquet garni and pour in the stock. Bring to the boil, reduce the heat and simmer for 1 hour, or until the lentils are tender.

Remove and discard the bouquet garni and season the soup to taste with pepper, and with salt, if necessary. Ladle into warmed soup bowls and serve immediately.

SERVES 4

450 g/1 lb thick, rindless smoked bacon rashers, diced

1 onion, chopped

2 carrots, sliced

2 celery sticks, chopped

1 turnip, chopped

1 large potato, chopped

85 g/3 oz Puy lentils

1 bouquet garni

1 litre/1¾ pints chicken stock

salt and pepper

CHEESE & BACON SOUP

Melt the butter in a large saucepan over a medium heat. Add the garlic and onion and cook, stirring, for 3 minutes, until slightly softened. Add the chopped bacon and leeks and cook for a further 3 minutes, stirring.

In a bowl, mix the flour with enough stock to make a smooth paste, then stir it into the pan. Cook, stirring, for 2 minutes. Pour in the remaining stock, then add the potatoes. Season with salt and pepper. Bring the soup to the boil, then lower the heat and simmer gently for 25 minutes, until the potatoes are tender and cooked through.

Stir in the cream and cook for 5 minutes, then gradually stir in the cheese until melted. Remove from the heat and ladle into serving bowls. Garnish with grated Cheddar cheese and serve immediately.

SERVES 4

- 2 tbsp butter
- 2 garlic cloves, chopped
- 1 large onion, sliced
- 250 g/9 oz smoked lean back bacon, chopped
- 2 large leeks, trimmed and sliced
- 2 tbsp plain flour
- 1 litre/1¾ pints vegetable stock
- 450 g/1 lb potatoes, chopped
- 100 ml/3½ fl oz double cream
- 300 g/10½ oz grated Cheddar cheese, plus extra to garnish
- salt and pepper

WONTON SOUP

SERVES 6–8

2 litres/3½ pints chicken stock

2 tsp salt

½ tsp white pepper

2 tbsp finely chopped spring onion, to serve

1 tbsp chopped fresh coriander leaves, to serve

wontons

175 g/6 oz minced pork, not too lean

225 g/8 oz raw prawns, peeled, deveined and chopped

½ tsp finely chopped fresh ginger

1 tbsp light soy sauce

1 tbsp Shaoxing rice wine

2 tsp finely chopped spring onion

pinch of sugar

pinch of white pepper

dash of sesame oil

30 square wonton wrappers

1 egg white, lightly beaten

For the wonton filling, mix together the pork, prawns, ginger, soy sauce, rice wine, spring onion, sugar, pepper and sesame oil, and stir well until the texture is thick and pasty. Set aside for at least 20 minutes.

To make the wontons, place a teaspoon of the filling at the centre of a wrapper. Brush the edges with a little egg white. Bring the opposite points towards each other and press the edges together, creating a flower-like shape. Repeat with the remaining wrappers and filling.

To make the soup, bring the stock to the boil and add the salt and pepper. Boil the wontons in the stock for about 5 minutes until the wrappers begin to wrinkle around the filling.

To serve, put the spring onion in individual bowls, spoon in the wontons and soup and top with the coriander.

SAUSAGE & RED CABBAGE SOUP

Heat the oil in a large saucepan. Add the garlic and onion and cook over a medium heat, stirring, for 3 minutes, until slightly softened. Add the leek and cook for a further 3 minutes, stirring.

In a bowl, mix the cornflour with enough stock to make a smooth paste, then stir it into the pan. Cook, stirring, for 2 minutes. Stir in the remaining stock, then add the potatoes and sausages. Season with salt and pepper. Bring to the boil, then lower the heat and simmer for 25 minutes.

Add the red cabbage and beans and cook for 10 minutes, then stir in the cream and cook for a further 5 minutes. Remove from the heat and ladle into serving bowls. Garnish with ground paprika and serve immediately.

SERVES 4

- 2 tbsp olive oil
- 1 garlic clove, chopped
- 1 large onion, chopped
- 1 large leek, sliced
- 2 tbsp cornflour
- 1 litre/1¾ pints vegetable stock
- 450 g/1 lb potatoes, sliced
- 200 g/7 oz skinless sausages, sliced
- 150 g/5½ oz red cabbage, chopped
- 200 g/7 oz canned black-eyed beans, drained
- 125 ml/4 fl oz double cream
- salt and pepper
- ground paprika, to garnish

ASIAN
LAMB SOUP

Trim all visible fat from the lamb and slice the meat thinly. Cut
the slices into bite-sized pieces. Spread the meat in one layer on
a plate and sprinkle over the garlic and 1 tablespoon of the soy
sauce. Leave to marinate, covered, for at least 10 minutes or up
to 1 hour.

Put the stock in a saucepan with the ginger, lemon grass,
remaining soy sauce and the chilli purée. Bring just to the boil,
reduce the heat, cover and simmer for 10–15 minutes.

When ready to serve the soup, drop the tomatoes, spring
onions, beansprouts and fresh coriander leaves into the
simmering stock.

Heat the oil in a frying pan and add the lamb with its marinade.
Stir-fry the lamb just until it is no longer red and divide among
warmed bowls.

Ladle over the hot stock and serve immediately.

SERVES 4

150 g/5½ oz lean tender lamb,
   such as neck fillet or leg steak

2 garlic cloves, very finely
   chopped

2 tbsp soy sauce

1.2 litres/2 pints chicken stock

1 tbsp grated fresh ginger

5-cm/2-inch piece lemon grass,
   sliced into very thin rounds

¼ tsp chilli purée, or to taste

6–8 cherry tomatoes, quartered

4 spring onions, finely sliced

50 g/1¾ oz beansprouts, snapped
   in half

2 tbsp fresh coriander leaves

1 tsp olive oil

CREAM OF CHICKEN SOUP

SERVES 4

3 tbsp butter

4 shallots, chopped

1 leek, sliced

450 g/1 lb skinless chicken breasts, chopped

600 ml/1 pint chicken stock

1 tbsp chopped fresh parsley

1 tbsp chopped fresh thyme, plus extra sprigs to garnish

175 ml/6 fl oz double cream

salt and pepper

Melt the butter in a large saucepan over a medium heat. Add the shallots and cook, stirring, for 3 minutes, until slightly softened. Add the leek and cook for a further 5 minutes, stirring. Add the chicken, stock and herbs, and season with salt and pepper. Bring to the boil, then lower the heat and simmer for 25 minutes, until the chicken is tender and cooked through. Remove from the heat and leave to cool for 10 minutes.

Transfer the soup to a food processor or blender and process until smooth (you may need to do this in batches). Return the soup to the rinsed-out pan and warm over a low heat for 5 minutes.

Stir in the cream and cook for a further 2 minutes, then remove from the heat and ladle into serving bowls. Garnish with sprigs of thyme and serve immediately.

CHICKEN-NOODLE SOUP

Put the chicken breasts and water in a saucepan over a high heat and bring to the boil. Lower the heat to its lowest setting and simmer, skimming the surface until no more foam rises. Add the onion, garlic, ginger, peppercorns, cloves, star anise and a pinch of salt, and continue to simmer for 20 minutes, or until the chicken is tender and cooked through. Meanwhile, grate the carrot along its length on the coarse side of a grater so you get long, thin strips.

Strain the chicken, reserving about 1.2 litres/2 pints stock, but discarding any flavouring solids. (At this point you can leave the stock to cool and refrigerate overnight, so any fat solidifies and can be lifted off and discarded.) Return the stock to the rinsed-out saucepan with the carrot, celery, baby sweetcorn and spring onions and bring to the boil. Boil until the baby sweetcorn are almost tender, then add the noodles and continue boiling for 2 minutes.

Meanwhile, chop the chicken, add to the pan and continue cooking for about 1 minute longer until the chicken is reheated and the noodles are soft. Add seasoning to taste.

SERVES 4–6

2 skinless chicken breasts

2 litres/3½ pints water

1 onion, unpeeled, halved

1 large garlic clove, halved

1-cm/½-inch piece fresh ginger, peeled and sliced

4 black peppercorns, lightly crushed

4 cloves

2 star anise

1 carrot, peeled

1 celery stick, chopped

100 g/3½ oz baby sweetcorn, halved lengthways

2 spring onions, finely shredded

115 g/4 oz dried rice vermicelli noodles

salt and pepper

COCK-A-LEEKIE SOUP

SERVES 6–8

2 tbsp olive oil

2 onions, roughly chopped

2 carrots, roughly chopped

5 leeks, 2 roughly chopped, 3 thinly sliced

1 chicken, weighing 1.3 kg/3 lb

2 bay leaves

6 prunes, sliced

salt and pepper

sprigs of fresh parsley, to garnish

Heat the oil in a large saucepan over a medium heat, then add the onions, carrots and the 2 roughly chopped leeks. Sauté for 3–4 minutes until just golden brown.

Wipe the chicken inside and out and remove any excess skin and fat.

Place the chicken in the saucepan with the cooked vegetables and add the bay leaves. Pour in enough cold water to just cover and season well with salt and pepper. Bring to the boil, reduce the heat, then cover and simmer for 1–1½ hours. From time to time skim off any scum that forms.

Remove the chicken from the stock, remove and discard the skin, then remove all the meat. Cut the meat into neat pieces.

Strain the stock through a colander, discard the vegetables and bay leaves and return to the rinsed-out saucepan. Expect to have 1.2–1.4 litres/2–2½ pints of stock. If you have time, it is a good idea to allow the stock to cool so that the fat may be removed. If not, blot the fat off the surface with pieces of kitchen paper.

Heat the stock to simmering point, add the sliced leeks and prunes to the saucepan and heat for about 1 minute.

Return the chicken to the pan and heat through. Serve immediately in warmed deep dishes. Garnish with the parsley.

CHICKEN & POTATO SOUP WITH BACON

tbsp butter

garlic cloves, chopped

onion, sliced

50 g/9 oz smoked lean back
bacon, chopped

large leeks, sliced

tbsp plain flour

itre/1¾ pints chicken stock

00 g/1 lb 12 oz potatoes,
chopped

00 g/7 oz skinless chicken
breast, chopped

tbsp double cream

lt and pepper

illed bacon and sprigs of fresh
flat-leaf parsley, to garnish

Melt the butter in a large saucepan over a medium heat. Add the garlic and onion and cook, stirring, for 3 minutes, until slightly softened. Add the chopped bacon and leeks and cook for a further 3 minutes, stirring.

In a bowl, mix the flour with enough stock to make a smooth paste, then stir it into the pan. Cook, stirring, for 2 minutes. Pour in the remaining stock, then add the potatoes and chicken. Season with salt and pepper. Bring to the boil, then lower the heat and simmer for 25 minutes, until the chicken and potatoes are tender and cooked through.

Stir in the cream and cook for a further 2 minutes, then remove from the heat and ladle into serving bowls. Garnish with the grilled bacon and flat-leaf parsley, and serve immediately.

CHICKEN GUMBO SOUP

Heat the oil in a large heavy-based saucepan over a medium-high heat and stir in the flour. Cook for about 15 minutes, stirring occasionally, until the mixture is a rich golden brown.

Add the onion, green pepper and celery and continue cooking for about 10 minutes until the onion softens.

Slowly pour in the stock and bring to the boil, stirring well and scraping the bottom of the pan to mix in the flour. Remove the pan from the heat.

Add the tomatoes and garlic. Stir in the okra and rice and season to taste with salt and pepper. Reduce the heat, cover and simmer for 20 minutes, or until the okra is tender.

Add the chicken and sausage and continue simmering for about 10 minutes. Taste and adjust the seasoning, if necessary, and ladle into warmed bowls to serve.

SERVES 6

2 tbsp olive oil

4 tbsp plain flour

1 onion, finely chopped

1 small green pepper, deseeded and finely chopped

1 celery stick, finely chopped

1.2 litres/2 pints chicken stock

400 g/14 oz canned chopped tomatoes

3 garlic cloves, finely chopped or crushed

125 g/4½ oz okra, stems removed, cut into 5-mm/¼-inch thick slices

50 g/1¾ oz white rice

200 g/7 oz cooked chicken, cubed

115 g/4 oz cooked garlic sausage, sliced or cubed

salt and pepper

THAI CHICKEN-COCONUT SOUP

Soak the dried noodles in a large bowl with enough lukewarm water to cover for 20 minutes, until soft. Alternatively, cook according to the packet instructions. Drain well and set aside.

Meanwhile, bring the stock to the boil in a large saucepan over a high heat. Lower the heat, add the lemon grass, ginger, lime leaves and chilli and simmer for 5 minutes. Add the chicken and continue simmering for a further 3 minutes, or until cooked. Stir in the coconut cream, nam pla and lime juice and continue simmering for 3 minutes. Add the beansprouts and spring onions and simmer for a further 1 minute. Taste and gradually add extra nam pla or lime juice at this point, if needed. Remove and discard the lemon grass stalk.

Divide the vermicelli noodles between 4 bowls. Bring the soup back to the boil, then add the soup to each bowl. The heat of the soup will warm the noodles. To garnish, sprinkle with coriander leaves.

SERVES 4

- 115 g/4 oz dried cellophane noodles
- 1.2 litres/2 pints chicken or vegetable stock
- 1 lemon grass stalk, crushed
- 1-cm/½-inch piece fresh ginger, peeled and very finely chopped
- 2 fresh kaffir lime leaves, thinly sliced
- 1 fresh red chilli, or to taste, deseeded and thinly sliced
- 2 skinless, boneless chicken breasts, thinly sliced
- 200 ml/7 fl oz coconut cream
- 2 tbsp nam pla (Thai fish sauce)
- 1 tbsp fresh lime juice
- 55 g/2 oz beansprouts
- 4 spring onions, green part only, finely sliced
- fresh coriander leaves, to garnish

TURKEY &
LENTIL SOUP

SERVES 4

- tbsp olive oil
- garlic clove, chopped
- large onion, chopped
- 200 g/7 oz mushrooms, sliced
- red pepper, deseeded and chopped
- 5 tomatoes, peeled, deseeded and chopped
- 1.2 litres/2 pints chicken stock
- 150 ml/5 fl oz red wine
- 85 g/3 oz cauliflower florets
- carrot, chopped
- 200 g/7 oz red lentils
- 350 g/12 oz cooked turkey, chopped
- courgette, chopped
- tbsp shredded fresh basil
- salt and pepper
- sprigs of fresh basil, to garnish

Heat the oil in a large saucepan. Add the garlic and onion and cook over a medium heat, stirring, for 3 minutes, until slightly softened. Add the mushrooms, red pepper and tomatoes and cook for a further 5 minutes, stirring. Pour in the stock and red wine, then add the cauliflower, carrot and red lentils. Season to taste with salt and pepper. Bring to the boil, then lower the heat and simmer the soup gently for 25 minutes, until the vegetables are tender and cooked through.

Add the turkey and courgette to the pan and cook for 10 minutes. Stir in the shredded basil and cook for a further 5 minutes, then remove from the heat and ladle into serving bowls. Garnish with basil and serve immediately.

Soups

57

DUCK WITH SPRING ONION SOUP

Slash the skin of the duck 3 or 4 times with a sharp knife and rub in the curry paste. Cook the duck breasts, skin-side down, in a wok or frying pan over a high heat for 2–3 minutes. Turn over, reduce the heat and cook for a further 3–4 minutes, until cooked through. Lift out and slice thickly. Set aside and keep warm.

Meanwhile, heat the oil in a wok or large frying pan and stir-fry half the spring onions, the garlic, ginger, carrots and red pepper for 2–3 minutes. Pour in the stock and add the chilli sauce, soy sauce and mushrooms. Bring to the boil, lower the heat and simmer for 4–5 minutes.

Ladle the soup into warmed bowls, top with the duck slices and garnish with the remaining spring onions. Serve immediately.

SERVES 2

2 duck breasts, skin on

2 tbsp red curry paste

2 tbsp vegetable or groundnut oil

bunch of spring onions, chopped

2 garlic cloves, crushed

5-cm/2-inch piece fresh ginger, grated

2 carrots, thinly sliced

1 red pepper, deseeded and cut into strips

1 litre/1¼ pints chicken stock

2 tbsp sweet chilli sauce

3–4 tbsp Thai soy sauce

400 g/14 oz canned straw mushrooms, drained

SEAFOOD CHOWDER

Discard any mussels with broken shells or any that refuse to close when tapped. Rinse and pull off any beards. Put the mussels in a large, heavy-based saucepan. Cover tightly and cook over a high heat for about 4 minutes, or until the mussels open, shaking the pan occasionally. Discard any that remain closed. When they are cool enough to handle, remove the mussels from their shells and set aside.

Put the flour in a mixing bowl and very slowly whisk in enough of the stock to make a thick paste. Whisk in a little more stock to make a smooth liquid.

Melt the butter in a heavy-based saucepan over a medium–low heat. Add the onion, cover and cook for 3 minutes, stirring frequently, until it softens.

Add the remaining fish stock and bring to the boil. Slowly whisk in the flour mixture until well combined and bring back to the boil, whisking constantly. Add the mussel cooking liquid. Season with salt, if needed, and pepper. Reduce the heat and simmer, partially covered, for 15 minutes.

Add the fish and mussels and continue simmering, stirring occasionally, for about 5 minutes, or until the fish is cooked and begins to flake.

Stir in the prawns and cream. Taste and adjust the seasoning. Simmer for a few minutes longer to heat through. Ladle into warmed bowls, sprinkle with dill and serve.

SERVES 6

1 kg/2 lb 4 oz live mussels

4 tbsp plain flour

1.5 litres/2¾ pints fish stock

1 tbsp butter

1 large onion, finely chopped

350 g/12 oz skinless white fish fillets, such as cod, sole or haddock

200 g/7 oz cooked or raw peeled prawns

300 ml/10 fl oz whipping cream or double cream

salt and pepper

snipped fresh dill, to garnish

BOUILLABAISSE

SERVES 4

400 ml/3½ fl oz olive oil

3 garlic cloves, chopped

2 onions, chopped

2 tomatoes, deseeded and
 chopped

700 ml/1¼ pints fish stock

400 ml/14 fl oz white wine

1 bay leaf

pinch of saffron threads

2 tbsp chopped fresh basil

2 tbsp chopped fresh parsley

200 g/7 oz live mussels

250 g/9 oz snapper or
 monkfish fillets

250 g/9 oz haddock fillets,
 skinned

200 g/7 oz prawns, peeled and
 deveined

100 g/3½ oz scallops

salt and pepper

Heat the oil in a large pan over a medium heat. Add the garlic
and onions and cook, stirring, for 3 minutes. Stir in the tomatoes,
stock, wine, bay leaf, saffron and herbs. Bring to the boil, reduce
the heat, cover and simmer for 30 minutes.

Meanwhile, soak the mussels in lightly salted water for
10 minutes. Scrub the shells under cold running water and pull
off any beards. Discard any mussels with broken shells or any
that refuse to close when tapped. Put the rest into a large pan
with a little water, bring to the boil and cook over a high heat
for 4 minutes. Remove from the heat and discard any that
remain closed.

When the tomato mixture is cooked, rinse the fish fillets,
pat dry and cut into chunks. Add to the pan and simmer for
5 minutes. Add the mussels, prawns and scallops and season
with salt and pepper. Cook for 3 minutes, until the fish is cooked
through. Remove from the heat, discard the bay leaf and ladle
into serving bowls.

SALMON & LEEK SOUP

Heat the oil in a heavy-based saucepan over a medium heat. Add the onion and leeks and cook for about 3 minutes until they begin to soften.

Add the potato, stock, water and bay leaf with a large pinch of salt. Bring to the boil, reduce the heat, cover and cook gently for about 25 minutes until the vegetables are tender. Remove the bay leaf.

Allow the soup to cool slightly, then transfer about half of it to a food processor or blender and process until smooth. (If using a food processor, strain off the cooking liquid and reserve. Purée half the soup solids with enough cooking liquid to moisten them, then combine with the remaining liquid.)

Return the puréed soup to the saucepan and stir to blend. Reheat gently over a medium–low heat.

Season the salmon with salt and pepper and add to the soup. Continue cooking for about 5 minutes, stirring occasionally, until the fish is tender and starts to break up. Stir in the cream, taste and adjust the seasoning, adding a little lemon juice, if using. Ladle into warmed bowls, garnish with chervil or parsley and serve.

SERVES 4

1 tbsp olive oil

1 large onion, finely chopped

3 large leeks, including green parts, thinly sliced

1 potato, finely diced

450 ml/16 fl oz fish stock

700 ml/1¼ pints water

1 bay leaf

300 g/10½ oz skinless salmon fillet, cut into 1-cm/½-inch cubes

80 ml/3 fl oz double cream

fresh lemon juice (optional)

salt and pepper

sprigs of fresh chervil or parsley, to garnish

THAI-STYLE SEAFOOD SOUP

Put the stock in a saucepan with the lemon grass, lime rind, ginger and chilli purée. Bring just to the boil, reduce the heat, cover and simmer for 10–15 minutes.

Cut the prawns almost in half lengthways, keeping the tail intact.

Strain the stock, return to the saucepan and bring to a simmer. Add the spring onions and cook for 2–3 minutes. Taste and season with salt, if needed, and stir in a little more chilli purée if wished.

Add the scallops and prawns and poach for about 1 minute until they turn opaque and the prawns curl.

Stir in the fresh coriander leaves, ladle the soup into warmed bowls, dividing the shellfish evenly, and garnish with chillies.

SERVES 4

1.2 litres/2 pints fish stock

1 lemon grass stalk, split lengthways

pared rind of ½ lime, or 1 lime leaf

2.5-cm/1-inch piece fresh ginger, sliced

¼ tsp chilli purée, or to taste

200 g/7 oz large or medium raw prawns, peeled

4–6 spring onions, sliced

250 g/9 oz scallops

2 tbsp fresh coriander leaves

salt

finely chopped red chillies, to garnish

GENOESE FISH SOUP

SERVES 6

- 25 g/1 oz butter
- 1 onion, chopped
- 1 garlic clove, finely chopped
- 55 g/2 oz rindless streaky bacon, diced
- 2 celery sticks, chopped
- 400 g/14 oz canned chopped tomatoes
- 150 ml/5 fl oz dry white wine
- 300 ml/10 fl oz fish stock
- 4 fresh basil leaves, torn
- 2 tbsp chopped fresh flat-leaf parsley
- 450 g/1 lb white fish fillets, such as cod or monkfish, skinned and chopped
- 115 g/4 oz cooked peeled prawns
- salt and pepper

Melt the butter in a large, heavy-based saucepan. Add the onion and garlic and cook over a low heat, stirring occasionally, for 5 minutes, or until softened.

Add the streaky bacon and celery and cook, stirring frequently, for a further 2 minutes.

Add the tomatoes, wine, stock, basil and 1 tablespoon of the parsley. Season to taste with salt and pepper. Bring to the boil, then reduce the heat and simmer for 10 minutes.

Add the fish and cook for 5 minutes, or until it is opaque. Add the prawns and heat through gently for 3 minutes. Ladle into warmed serving bowls, garnish with the remaining chopped parsley and serve immediately.

SOUPS

SWEETCORN & CRAB SOUP

Heat the oil in a large frying pan and fry the garlic, shallots, lemon grass and ginger over a low heat, stirring occasionally, for 2–3 minutes, until softened. Add the stock and coconut milk and bring to the boil. Add the sweetcorn, lower the heat and simmer gently for 3–4 minutes.

Add the crabmeat, fish sauce, lime juice and sugar and simmer gently for 1 minute. Ladle into warmed bowls, garnish with the chopped coriander and serve immediately.

SERVES 6

2 tbsp vegetable or groundnut oil

4 garlic cloves, finely chopped

5 shallots, finely chopped

2 lemon grass stalks, finely chopped

2.5-cm/1-inch piece fresh ginger, finely chopped

1 litre/1¾ pints chicken stock

400 g/14 oz canned coconut milk

225 g/8 oz frozen sweetcorn kernels

350 g/12 oz canned crabmeat, drained and shredded

2 tbsp fish sauce

juice of 1 lime

1 tsp palm sugar or soft light brown sugar

bunch of fresh coriander, chopped, to garnish

CLAM & CORN CHOWDER

Melt the butter in a large saucepan over a medium–low heat. Add the onion and carrot and cook for 3–4 minutes, stirring frequently, until the onion is softened. Stir in the flour and continue cooking for 2 minutes.

Slowly add about half the stock and stir well, scraping the bottom of the pan to mix in the flour. Pour in the remaining stock and the water and bring just to the boil, stirring.

Add the potatoes, sweetcorn and milk and stir to combine. Reduce the heat and simmer gently, partially covered, for about 20 minutes, stirring occasionally, until all the vegetables are tender.

Chop the clams, if large. Stir in the clams and continue cooking for about 5 minutes until heated through. Taste and adjust the seasoning, if needed.

Ladle the soup into bowls and sprinkle with parsley.

SERVES 4

4 tsp butter

1 large onion, finely chopped

1 small carrot, finely diced

3 tbsp plain flour

300 ml/10 fl oz fish stock

200 ml/7 fl oz water

450 g/1 lb potatoes, diced

125 g/4 oz cooked or defrosted frozen sweetcorn

450 ml/16 fl oz milk

280 g/10 oz canned clams, drained and rinsed

salt and pepper

chopped fresh parsley, to garnish

MEAT

POT ROAST WITH POTATOES & DILL

Preheat the oven to 140°C/275°F/Gas Mark 1. Mix 2 tablespoons of the flour with the salt and pepper in a shallow dish. Dip the meat to coat. Heat the oil in a flameproof casserole and brown the meat all over. Transfer to a plate. Add half the butter to the casserole and cook the onion, celery, carrots, dill seed and thyme for 5 minutes. Return the meat and juices to the casserole.

Pour in the wine and enough stock to reach one third of the way up the meat. Bring to the boil, cover and cook in the oven for 3 hours, turning the meat every 30 minutes. After it has been cooking for 2 hours, add the potatoes and more stock if necessary.

When ready, transfer the meat and vegetables to a warmed serving dish. Strain the cooking liquid to remove any solids, then return the liquid to the casserole.

Mix the remaining butter and flour to a paste. Bring the cooking liquid to the boil. Whisk in small pieces of the flour and butter paste, whisking constantly until the sauce is smooth. Pour the sauce over the meat and vegetables. Sprinkle with the fresh dill to serve.

SERVES 6

- 2½ tbsp plain flour
- 1 tsp salt
- ¼ tsp pepper
- 1 rolled brisket joint, weighing 1.6 kg/3 lb 8 oz
- 2 tbsp vegetable oil
- 2 tbsp butter
- 1 onion, finely chopped
- 2 celery sticks, diced
- 2 carrots, peeled and diced
- 1 tsp dill seed
- 1 tsp dried thyme or oregano
- 350 ml/12 fl oz red wine
- 150–225 ml/5–8 fl oz beef stock
- 4–5 potatoes, cut into large chunks and boiled until just tender
- 2 tbsp chopped fresh dill, to serve

BEEF
STROGANOFF

Place the dried ceps in a bowl and cover with hot water. Leave to soak for 20 minutes. Meanwhile, cut the beef against the grain into 5-mm/¼-inch thick slices, then into 1-cm/½-inch long strips, and reserve.

Drain the ceps, reserving the soaking liquid, and chop. Strain the soaking liquid through a fine-mesh sieve or coffee filter and reserve.

Heat half the oil in a large frying pan. Add the shallots and cook over a low heat, stirring occasionally, for 5 minutes, or until softened. Add the soaked ceps, reserved soaking water and whole chestnut mushrooms and cook, stirring frequently, for 10 minutes, or until almost all of the liquid has evaporated, then transfer the mixture to a plate.

Heat the remaining oil in the frying pan, add the beef and cook, stirring frequently, for 4 minutes, or until browned all over. You may need to do this in batches. Return the mushroom mixture to the frying pan and season to taste with salt and pepper. Place the mustard and cream in a small bowl and stir to mix, then fold into the meat and mushroom mixture. Heat through gently, then serve with freshly cooked pasta, garnished with chives.

SERVES 4

15 g/½ oz dried ceps

350 g/12 oz beef fillet

2 tbsp olive oil

115 g/4 oz shallots, sliced

175 g/6 oz chestnut mushrooms

½ tsp Dijon mustard

5 tbsp double cream

salt and pepper

freshly cooked pasta, to serve

fresh chives, to garnish

CHILLI CON CARNE

50 g/1 lb 10 oz lean
stewing steak

tbsp vegetable oil

large onion, sliced

–4 garlic cloves, crushed

tbsp plain flour

25 ml/15 fl oz tomato juice

00 g/14 oz canned tomatoes

–2 tbsp sweet chilli sauce

tsp ground cumin

25 g/15 oz canned red kidney
beans, drained and rinsed

teaspoon dried oregano

–2 tbsp chopped fresh parsley

alt and pepper

prigs of fresh herbs, to garnish

eshly cooked rice and tortillas,
to serve

Preheat the oven to 160°C/325°F/Gas Mark 3. Using a sharp
knife, cut the beef into 2-cm/¾-inch cubes. Heat the vegetable
oil in a large flameproof casserole dish and fry the beef over a
medium heat until well sealed on all sides. Remove the beef from
the casserole with a slotted spoon and reserve until required.

Add the onion and garlic to the casserole and fry until lightly
browned; then stir in the flour and cook for 1–2 minutes.

Stir in the tomato juice and tomatoes and bring to the boil.
Return the beef to the casserole and add the chilli sauce, cumin
and salt and pepper to taste. Cover and cook in the preheated
oven for 1½ hours, or until the beef is almost tender.

Stir in the kidney beans, oregano and parsley, and adjust the
seasoning to taste, if necessary. Cover the casserole and return
to the oven for 45 minutes. Serve on a bed of freshly cooked
rice, garnished with sprigs of fresh herbs and accompanied
by tortillas.

MEAT

81

BEEF GOULASH

Heat the vegetable oil in a large frying pan and cook the onion and garlic for 3–4 minutes.

Cut the steak into chunks and cook over a high heat for 3 minutes until browned all over. Add the paprika and stir well, then add the chopped tomatoes, tomato purée, red pepper and mushrooms. Cook for 2 minutes, stirring frequently.

Pour in the beef stock. Bring to the boil, then reduce the heat. Cover and simmer for 1½–2 hours until the meat is tender.

Blend the cornflour with the water, then add to the pan, stirring until thickened and smooth. Cook for 1 minute, then season with salt and pepper to taste.

Put the yogurt in a serving bowl and sprinkle with a little paprika.

Transfer the beef goulash to a warmed serving dish, garnish with chopped fresh parsley and serve with freshly cooked long-grain and wild rice.

SERVES 4

2 tbsp vegetable oil

1 large onion, chopped

1 garlic clove, crushed

750 g/1 lb 10 oz lean stewing steak

2 tbsp paprika

425 g/15 oz canned chopped tomatoes

2 tbsp tomato purée

1 large red pepper, deseeded and chopped

175 g/6 oz mushrooms, sliced

600 ml/1 pint beef stock

1 tbsp cornflour

1 tbsp water

4 tbsp natural yogurt

salt and pepper

paprika, for sprinkling

chopped fresh parsley, to garnish

freshly cooked long-grain and wild rice, to serve

BEEF WITH HERBS & VEGETABLES

Preheat the oven to 190°C/375°F/Gas Mark 5. To make the stock, trim as much fat as possible from the beef and put in a large roasting tin with the bones and onions. Roast in a preheated oven for 30–40 minutes until browned, turning once or twice. Transfer the ingredients to a large flameproof casserole and discard the fat.

Add the water (it should cover the meat by at least 5 cm/ 2 inches) and bring to the boil. Skim off any scum that rises to the surface. Reduce the heat and add the garlic, carrots, celery, bay leaf, thyme and a pinch of salt. Simmer very gently, uncovered, for 4 hours, skimming occasionally. Do not stir. If the ingredients emerge from the liquid, top up with water.

Gently ladle the stock through a muslin-lined sieve into a large container and remove as much fat as possible. Save the meat for another purpose, if wished, and discard the bones and vegetables. (There should be about 2 litres/3½ pints of stock.)

Boil the stock very gently until it is reduced to 1.5 litres/ 2¾ pints or, if the stock already has concentrated flavour, measure out that amount and save the rest for another purpose.

Bring a saucepan of salted water to the boil and drop in the celeriac and carrots. Reduce the heat, cover and boil gently for about 15 minutes until tender. Drain.

Add the marjoram and parsley to the boiling beef stock. Divide the cooked vegetables and diced tomatoes between warmed bowls, ladle over the boiling stock and serve.

SERVES 4–6

200 g/7 oz celeriac, peeled and finely diced

2 large carrots, finely diced

2 tsp chopped fresh marjoram leaves

2 tsp chopped fresh parsley

2 plum tomatoes, skinned, deseeded and diced

salt and pepper

beef stock

550 g/1 lb 4 oz boneless beef shin or stewing steak, cut into large cubes

750 g/1 lb 10 oz veal, beef or pork bones

2 onions, quartered

2.5 litres/4⅓ pints water

4 garlic cloves, sliced

2 carrots, sliced

1 celery stick, chopped

1 bay leaf

4–5 sprigs of fresh thyme or ¼ tsp dried thyme

salt

PEPPER POT-STYLE STEW

SERVES 4

450 g/1 lb braising beef steak

1½ tbsp plain flour

2 tbsp olive oil

1 Spanish onion, chopped

3–4 garlic cloves, crushed

1 fresh green chilli, deseeded and chopped

3 celery sticks, sliced

4 whole cloves

1 tsp ground allspice

1–2 teaspoons hot pepper sauce, or to taste

600 ml/1 pint beef stock

225 g/8 oz deseeded and peeled squash, such as acorn, cut into small chunks

1 large red pepper, deseeded and chopped

4 tomatoes, roughly chopped

115 g/4 oz okra, trimmed and halved

freshly cooked wild rice, to serve

Trim any fat or gristle from the beef and cut into 2.5-cm/1-inch chunks. Toss the beef in the flour until well coated and reserve any remaining flour.

Heat the oil in a large, heavy-based saucepan and cook the onion, garlic, chilli and celery with the cloves and allspice, stirring frequently, for 5 minutes, or until softened. Add the beef and cook over a high heat, stirring frequently, for 3 minutes, or until browned on all sides and sealed. Sprinkle in the reserved flour and cook, stirring constantly, for 2 minutes, then remove from the heat.

Add the hot pepper sauce and gradually stir in the stock, then return to the heat and bring to the boil, stirring. Reduce the heat, cover and simmer, stirring occasionally, for 1½ hours.

Add the squash and red pepper to the saucepan and simmer for a further 15 minutes. Add the tomatoes and okra and simmer for a further 15 minutes, or until the beef is tender. Serve with the wild rice.

BEEF &
VEGETABLE
STEW

Trim any fat or gristle from the beef and cut into 2.5-cm/1-inch chunks. Mix the flour and spices together. Toss the beef in the spiced flour until well coated.

Heat the oil in a large, heavy-based saucepan and cook the onion, garlic and celery, stirring frequently, for 5 minutes, or until softened. Add the beef and cook over a high heat, stirring frequently, for 3 minutes, or until browned on all sides and sealed.

Add the carrots, then remove from the heat. Gradually stir in the lager and stock, then return to the heat and bring to the boil, stirring. Reduce the heat, cover and simmer, stirring occasionally, for 1½ hours.

Add the potatoes to the saucepan and simmer for a further 15 minutes. Add the red pepper and corn on the cob and simmer for a further 15 minutes, then add the tomatoes and peas and simmer for a further 10 minutes, or until the beef and vegetables are tender. Season to taste with salt and pepper, stir in the coriander and serve.

SERVES 4

450 g/1 lb braising steak

1½ tbsp plain flour

1 tsp hot paprika

1–1½ tsp chilli powder

1 tsp ground ginger

2 tbsp olive oil

1 large onion, cut into chunks

3 garlic cloves, sliced

2 celery sticks, sliced

225 g/8 oz carrots, chopped

300 ml/10 fl oz lager

300 ml/10 fl oz beef stock

350 g/12 oz potatoes, chopped

1 red pepper, deseeded and chopped

2 corn on the cob, halved

115 g/4 oz tomatoes, quartered

115 g/4 oz shelled fresh or frozen peas

1 tbsp chopped fresh coriander

salt and pepper

DAUBE OF BEEF

Combine the wine, brandy, vinegar, shallots, carrots, garlic, peppercorns, thyme, rosemary, parsley and bay leaf, and season to taste with salt. Add the beef, stirring to coat, then cover with clingfilm and leave in the refrigerator to marinate for 8 hours, or overnight.

Preheat the oven to 150°C/300°F/Gas Mark 2. Drain the beef, reserving the marinade, and pat dry on kitchen paper. Heat half the oil in a large, flameproof casserole. Add the beef in batches and cook over a medium heat, stirring, for 3–4 minutes, or until browned. Transfer the beef to a plate with a slotted spoon. Brown the remaining beef, adding more oil, if necessary.

Return all of the beef to the casserole and add the tomatoes and their juices, mushrooms and orange rind. Strain the reserved marinade into the casserole. Bring to the boil, cover and cook in the oven for 2½ hours.

Remove the casserole from the oven, add the ham and olives and return it to the oven to cook for a further 30 minutes, or until the beef is very tender. Discard the orange rind and serve straight from the casserole, garnished with parsley.

SERVES 6

350 ml/12 fl oz dry white wine

2 tbsp brandy

1 tbsp white wine vinegar

4 shallots, sliced

4 carrots, sliced

1 garlic clove, finely chopped

6 black peppercorns

4 fresh thyme sprigs

1 fresh rosemary sprig

2 fresh parsley sprigs, plus extra to garnish

1 bay leaf

750 g/1 lb 10 oz beef topside, cut into 2.5-cm/1-inch cubes

2 tbsp olive oil

800 g/1 lb 12 oz canned chopped tomatoes

225 g/8 oz mushrooms, sliced

strip of finely pared orange rind

55 g/2 oz Bayonne ham, cut into strips

12 black olives

salt

BEEF IN BEER WITH HERB DUMPLINGS

SERVES 6

2 tbsp sunflower oil

2 large onions, thinly sliced

8 carrots, sliced

4 tbsp plain flour

1.25 kg/2 lb 12 oz stewing steak, cut into cubes

425 ml/15 fl oz stout

2 tsp muscovado sugar

2 bay leaves

1 tbsp chopped fresh thyme

salt and pepper

herb dumplings

115 g/4 oz self-raising flour

pinch of salt

55 g/2 oz shredded suet

2 tbsp chopped fresh parsley, plus extra to garnish

about 4 tbsp water

Preheat the oven to 160°C/325°F/Gas Mark 3. Heat the oil in a flameproof casserole. Add the onions and carrots and cook over a low heat, stirring occasionally, for 5 minutes, or until the onions are softened. Meanwhile, place the flour in a polythene bag and season with salt and pepper. Add the stewing steak to the bag, tie the top and shake well to coat. Do this in batches, if necessary.

Remove the vegetables from the casserole with a slotted spoon and reserve. Add the stewing steak to the casserole, in batches, and cook, stirring frequently, until browned all over. Return all the meat and the onions and carrots to the casserole and sprinkle in any remaining seasoned flour. Pour in the stout and add the sugar, bay leaves and thyme. Bring to the boil, cover and transfer to the preheated oven to bake for 1¾ hours.

To make the herb dumplings, sift the flour and salt into a bowl. Stir in the suet and parsley and add enough of the water to make a soft dough. Shape into small balls between the palms of your hands. Add to the casserole and return to the oven for 30 minutes. Remove and discard the bay leaves. Serve immediately, sprinkled with chopped parsley.

BEEF CHOP SUEY

Combine all the marinade ingredients in a bowl and marinate the beef for at least 20 minutes. Blanch the broccoli in a large pan of boiling water for 30 seconds. Drain and set aside.

In a preheated wok or deep pan, heat 1 tablespoon of the oil and stir-fry the beef until the colour has changed. Remove and set aside. Wipe out the wok or pan with kitchen paper.

In the clean wok or deep pan, heat the remaining oil and stir-fry the onion for 1 minute. Add the celery and broccoli and cook for 2 minutes. Add the mangetout, bamboo shoots, water chestnuts and mushrooms and cook for 1 minute. Add the beef, season with the oyster sauce and salt and serve.

SERVES 4

- 450 g/1 lb ribeye or sirloin steak, thinly sliced
- 1 head of broccoli, cut into small florets
- 2 tbsp vegetable or groundnut oil
- 1 onion, thinly sliced
- 2 sticks celery, thinly sliced diagonally
- 225 g/8 oz mangetout, sliced in half lengthways
- 55 g/2 oz fresh or canned bamboo shoots, rinsed and julienned (if using fresh shoots, boil in water first for 30 minutes)
- 8 water chestnuts, thinly sliced
- 225 g/8 oz mushrooms, thinly sliced
- 1 tbsp oyster sauce
- 1 tsp salt

marinade
- 1 tbsp Shaoxing rice wine
- pinch of white pepper
- pinch of salt
- 1 tbsp light soy sauce
- ½ tsp sesame oil

POT-ROAST PORK

Heat the oil with half the butter in a heavy-based saucepan or flameproof casserole. Add the pork and cook over a medium heat, turning frequently, for 5–10 minutes, or until browned. Transfer to a plate.

Add the shallots to the saucepan and cook, stirring frequently, for 5 minutes, or until softened. Add the juniper berries and thyme sprigs and return the pork to the saucepan, with any juices that have collected on the plate. Pour in the cider and stock, season to taste with salt and pepper, then cover and simmer for 30 minutes. Turn the pork over and add the celery. Re-cover the pan and cook for a further 40 minutes.

Meanwhile, make a beurre manié by mashing the remaining butter with the flour in a small bowl. Transfer the pork to a platter with a slotted spoon and keep warm. Remove and discard the juniper berries and thyme. Whisk the beurre manié, a little at a time, into the simmering cooking liquid. Cook, stirring constantly, for 2 minutes, then stir in the cream and bring to the boil.

Slice the pork and spoon a little of the sauce over it. Garnish with thyme sprigs and serve immediately with freshly cooked peas and the remaining sauce.

SERVES 4

- 1 tbsp sunflower oil
- 55 g/2 oz butter
- 1 kg/2 lb 4 oz boned and rolled pork loin joint
- 4 shallots, chopped
- 6 juniper berries
- 2 fresh thyme sprigs, plus extra to garnish
- 150 ml/5 fl oz dry cider
- 150 ml/5 fl oz chicken stock or water
- 8 celery sticks, chopped
- 2 tbsp plain flour
- 150 ml/5 fl oz double cream
- salt and pepper
- freshly cooked peas, to serve

PORK &
VEGETABLE
BROTH

tbsp chilli oil

garlic clove, chopped

spring onions, sliced

red pepper, deseeded and
finely sliced

tbsp cornflour

litre/1¾ pints vegetable stock

tbsp soy sauce

tbsp rice wine or dry sherry

50 g/5½ oz pork fillet, sliced

tbsp finely chopped lemon grass

small red chilli, deseeded and
finely chopped

tbsp grated fresh ginger

15 g/4 oz fine egg noodles

00 g/7 oz canned water
chestnuts, drained and sliced

salt and pepper

Heat the oil in a large saucepan. Add the garlic and spring
onions and cook over a medium heat, stirring, for 3 minutes,
until slightly softened. Add the red pepper and cook for a
further 5 minutes, stirring.

In a bowl, mix the cornflour with enough of the stock to make
a smooth paste, then stir it into the pan. Cook, stirring, for
2 minutes. Stir in the remaining stock and the soy sauce and
rice wine, then add the pork, lemon grass, chilli and ginger.
Season with salt and pepper. Bring to the boil, then lower the
heat and simmer for 25 minutes.

Bring a separate saucepan of water to the boil, add the noodles
and cook for 3 minutes. Remove from the heat, drain, then add
the noodles to the soup along with the water chestnuts. Cook
for a further 2 minutes, then remove from the heat and ladle into
serving bowls.

PORK CHOPS WITH PEPPERS & SWEETCORN

Heat the oil in a large, flameproof casserole. Add the pork chops in batches and cook over a medium heat, turning occasionally, for 5 minutes, or until browned. Transfer the chops to a plate with a slotted spoon.

Add the chopped onion to the casserole and cook, stirring occasionally, for 5 minutes, or until softened. Add the garlic and peppers and cook, stirring occasionally for a further 5 minutes. Stir in the sweetcorn kernels with their juices and the parsley, and season to taste with salt and pepper.

Return the chops to the casserole, spooning the vegetable mixture over them. Cover and simmer for 30 minutes, or until tender. Serve immediately with mashed potatoes.

SERVES 4

1 tbsp sunflower oil

4 pork chops, trimmed of visible fat

1 onion, chopped

1 garlic clove, finely chopped

1 green pepper, deseeded and sliced

1 red pepper, deseeded and sliced

325 g/11½ oz canned sweetcorn kernels

1 tbsp chopped fresh parsley

salt and pepper

mashed potatoes, to serve

PORK & VEGETABLE RAGOUT

Trim off any fat or gristle from the pork and cut into thin strips about 5 cm/2 inches long. Mix the flour and spices together. Toss the pork in the spiced flour until well coated and reserve any remaining spiced flour.

Heat the oil in a large, heavy-based saucepan and cook the onion, stirring frequently, for 5 minutes, or until softened. Add the pork and cook over a high heat, stirring frequently, for 5 minutes, or until browned on all sides and sealed. Sprinkle in the reserved spiced flour and cook, stirring constantly, for 2 minutes, then remove from the heat.

Gradually add the tomatoes to the saucepan. Blend the tomato purée with a little of the stock in a jug and gradually stir into the saucepan, then stir in half the remaining stock.

Add the carrots, then return to the heat and bring to the boil, stirring. Reduce the heat, cover and simmer, stirring occasionally, for 1½ hours. Add the squash and cook for a further 15 minutes.

Add the leeks and okra, and the remaining stock if you prefer a thinner ragout. Simmer for a further 15 minutes, or until the pork and vegetables are tender. Season to taste with salt and pepper, then garnish with fresh parsley and serve with couscous.

SERVES 4

450 g/1 lb lean boneless pork

1½ tbsp plain flour

1 tsp ground coriander

1 tsp ground cumin

1½ tsp ground cinnamon

1 tbsp olive oil

1 onion, chopped

400 g/14 oz canned chopped tomatoes

2 tbsp tomato purée

300–450 ml/10–16 fl oz chicken stock

225 g/8 oz carrots, chopped

350 g/12 oz squash, such as kabocha, peeled, deseeded and chopped

225 g/8 oz leeks, sliced, blanched and drained

115 g/4 oz okra, trimmed and sliced

salt and pepper

fresh parsley sprigs, to garnish

couscous, to serve

PORK WITH RED CABBAGE

SERVES 4

1 tbsp sunflower oil

750 g/1 lb 10 oz boned and rolled
   pork loin joint

1 onion, finely chopped

500 g/1 lb 2 oz red cabbage,
   thick stems removed and leaves
   shredded

2 large cooking apples, peeled,
   cored and sliced

3 cloves

1 tsp brown sugar

3 tbsp lemon juice, and a thinly
   pared strip of lemon rind

lemon wedges, to garnish

Preheat the oven to 160°C/325°F/Gas Mark 3. Heat the oil in
a flameproof casserole. Add the pork and cook over a medium
heat, turning frequently, for 5–10 minutes, or until browned.
Transfer to a plate.

Add the chopped onion to the casserole and cook over a low
heat, stirring occasionally, for 5 minutes, or until softened.
Add the cabbage, in batches, and cook, stirring, for 2 minutes.
Transfer each batch (mixed with some onion) into a bowl with a
slotted spoon.

Add the apple slices, cloves and sugar to the bowl and mix
well, then place about half the mixture in the base of the
casserole. Top with the pork and add the remaining cabbage
mixture. Sprinkle in the lemon juice and add the strip of rind.
Cover and cook in the preheated oven for 1½ hours.

Transfer the pork to a plate. Transfer the cabbage mixture to
the plate with a slotted spoon and keep warm. Bring the cooking
juices to the boil over a high heat and reduce slightly. Slice the
pork and arrange on warmed serving plates, surrounded by the
cabbage mixture. Spoon the cooking juices over the meat and
serve, garnished with wedges of lemon.

PAPRIKA PORK

Cut the pork into 4-cm/ 1½-inch cubes. Heat the oil and butter in a large saucepan. Add the pork and cook over a medium heat, stirring, for 5 minutes, or until browned. Transfer to a plate with a slotted spoon.

Add the chopped onion to the saucepan and cook, stirring occasionally, for 5 minutes, or until softened. Stir in the paprika and flour and cook, stirring constantly, for 2 minutes. Gradually stir in the stock and bring to the boil, stirring constantly.

Return the pork to the saucepan, add the sherry and sliced mushrooms and season to taste with salt and pepper. Cover and simmer gently for 20 minutes, or until the pork is tender. Stir in the soured cream and serve.

SERVES 4

675 g/1 lb 8 oz pork fillet
2 tbsp sunflower oil
25 g/1 oz butter
1 onion, chopped
1 tbsp paprika
25 g/1 oz plain flour
300 ml/10 fl oz chicken stock
4 tbsp dry sherry
115 g/4 oz mushrooms, sliced
salt and pepper
150 ml/5 fl oz soured cream

SAUSAGE & BEAN CASSEROLE

Prick the sausages all over with a fork. Heat 2 tablespoons of the oil in a large, heavy frying pan. Add the sausages and cook over a low heat, turning frequently, for 10–15 minutes, until evenly browned and cooked through. Remove them from the frying pan and keep warm. Drain off the oil and wipe out the pan with kitchen paper.

Heat the remaining oil in the frying pan. Add the onion, garlic and pepper to the frying pan and cook for 5 minutes, stirring occasionally, or until softened.

Add the tomatoes to the frying pan and leave the mixture to simmer for about 5 minutes, stirring occasionally, or until slightly reduced and thickened.

Stir the sun-dried tomato paste, cannellini beans and Italian sausages into the mixture in the frying pan. Cook for 4–5 minutes or until the mixture is piping hot. Add 4–5 tablespoons of water, if the mixture becomes too dry during cooking.

Transfer to serving plates and serve with mashed potatoes.

SERVES 4

8 Italian sausages

3 tbsp olive oil

1 large onion, chopped

2 garlic cloves, chopped

1 green bell pepper, deseeded and sliced

225g/8 oz canned chopped tomatoes, skinned and chopped or 400 g/14 oz can tomatoes, chopped

2 tbsp sun-dried tomato paste

400 g/14 oz canned cannellini beans

mashed potatoes or rice, to serve

ASIAN PORK

450 g/1 lb lean boneless pork
1½ tbsp plain flour
1–2 tbsp olive oil
1 onion, cut into small wedges
2–3 garlic cloves, chopped
2.5-cm/1-inch piece fresh ginger, peeled and grated
1 tbsp tomato purée
300 ml/10 fl oz chicken stock
225 g/8 oz canned pineapple chunks in natural juice
1–1½ tbsp dark soy sauce
1 red pepper, deseeded and sliced
1 green pepper, deseeded and sliced
1½ tbsp balsamic vinegar
4 spring onions, diagonally sliced, to garnish

Trim off any fat or gristle from the pork and cut into 2.5-cm/1-inch chunks. Toss the pork in the flour until well coated and reserve any remaining flour.

Heat the oil in a large, heavy-based saucepan and cook the onion, garlic and ginger, stirring frequently, for 5 minutes, or until softened. Add the pork and cook over a high heat, stirring frequently, for 5 minutes, or until browned on all sides and sealed. Sprinkle in the reserved flour and cook, stirring constantly, for 2 minutes, then remove from the heat.

Blend the tomato purée with the stock in a heatproof jug and gradually stir into the saucepan. Remove the pineapple chunks from their juice and stir the juice into the saucepan.

Add the soy sauce to the saucepan, then return to the heat and bring to the boil, stirring. Reduce the heat, cover and simmer, stirring occasionally, for 1 hour. Add the peppers and cook for a further 15 minutes, or until the pork is tender. Stir in the vinegar and the pineapple and heat through for 5 minutes. Serve sprinkled with the spring onions.

MEAT

111

RED CURRY PORK WITH PEPPERS

Heat the oil in a wok or large frying pan and fry the onion and garlic for 1–2 minutes, until they are softened but not browned.

Add the pork slices and stir-fry for 2–3 minutes until browned all over. Add the pepper, mushrooms and curry paste.

Dissolve the coconut in the stock and add to the wok with the soy sauce. Bring to the boil and simmer for 4–5 minutes until the liquid has reduced and thickened.

Add the tomatoes and coriander and cook for 1–2 minutes before serving with noodles.

SERVES 4

2 tbsp vegetable or groundnut oil

1 onion, roughly chopped

2 garlic cloves, chopped

450 g/1 lb pork fillet, thickly sliced

1 red pepper, deseeded and cut into squares

175 g/6 oz mushrooms, quartered

2 tbsp Thai red curry paste

115 g/4 oz creamed coconut, chopped

300 ml/½ pint pork or vegetable stock

2 tbsp Thai soy sauce

4 tomatoes, peeled, deseeded and chopped

handful of fresh coriander, chopped

boiled noodles or rice, to serve

LAMB SHANKS
WITH HARISSA

Preheat the oven to 200°C/400°F/Gas Mark 6. Prick the aubergines, place on a baking sheet and bake for 1 hour. When cool, peel and chop.

Heat the oil in a saucepan. Add the lamb and cook until browned. Add the onion, stock and water. Bring to the boil. Reduce the heat and simmer for 1 hour.

For the harissa, process the peppers, coriander seeds, chillies, garlic and caraway seeds in a food processor. With the motor running, add enough oil to make a paste. Add salt to taste, then spoon into a bowl.

Remove the shanks from the stock, cut off the meat and chop. Add the sweet potato, cinnamon stick and cumin to the stock, bring to the boil, cover and simmer for 20 minutes. Discard the cinnamon and process the mixture in a food processor with the aubergine. Return to the saucepan, add the lamb and coriander and heat until hot. Serve with the harissa.

SERVES 4

2 aubergines

3 tbsp olive oil

6 lamb shanks

1 small onion, chopped

400 ml/14 fl oz chicken stock

2 litres/3½ pints water

400 g/14 oz sweet potato, cut into chunks

5-cm/2-inch piece cinnamon stick

1 tsp ground cumin

2 tbsp chopped fresh coriander

harissa

2 red peppers, roasted, peeled, deseeded and chopped

½ tsp coriander seeds, dry-fried

25 g/1 oz fresh red chillies, chopped

2 garlic cloves, chopped

2 tsp caraway seeds

olive oil

salt

AZERBAIJANI LAMB PILAU

SERVES 4

2–3 tbsp vegetable oil

550 g/1 lb 7 oz boneless lamb
  shoulder, cut into 2.5-cm/1-inch
  cubes

2 onions, roughly chopped

1 tsp ground cumin

200 g/7 oz arborio rice

1 tbsp tomato purée

1 tsp saffron threads

100 ml/3½ fl oz pomegranate
  juice

850 ml/1½ pints lamb stock,
  chicken stock or water

115 g/4 oz ready-to-eat dried
  apricots or prunes, halved

2 tbsp raisins

salt and pepper

2 tsp shredded fresh mint and
  2 tsp shredded fresh watercress,
  to garnish

Heat the oil in a large flameproof casserole or saucepan over a
high heat. Add the lamb, in batches, and cook over a high heat,
turning frequently, for 7 minutes, or until lightly browned.

Add the onions, reduce the heat to medium and cook for
2 minutes, or until beginning to soften. Add the cumin and
rice and cook, stirring to coat, for 2 minutes, or until the rice is
translucent. Stir in the tomato purée and the saffron threads.

Add the pomegranate juice and stock. Bring to the boil, stirring.
Stir in the apricots and raisins. Reduce the heat to low, cover, and
simmer for 20–25 minutes, or until the lamb and rice are tender
and all of the liquid has been absorbed.

Season to taste with salt and pepper, then sprinkle the
shredded mint and watercress over the pilau and serve straight
from the casserole.

LAMB WITH PEARS

Preheat the oven to 160°C/325°F/Gas Mark 3. Heat the olive oil in a flameproof casserole over a medium heat. Add the lamb and cook, turning frequently, for 5–10 minutes, or until browned on all sides.

Arrange the pear quarters on top, then sprinkle over the ginger. Cover with the potatoes. Pour in the cider and season to taste with salt and pepper. Cover and cook in the preheated oven for 1¼ hours.

Trim the stalk ends of the green beans. Remove the casserole from the oven and add the beans, then re-cover and return to the oven for a further 30 minutes. Taste and adjust the seasoning. Sprinkle with the chives and serve.

SERVES 4

1 tbsp olive oil

1 kg/2 lb 4 oz best end-of-neck lamb cutlets, trimmed of visible fat

6 pears, peeled, cored and quartered

1 tsp ground ginger

4 potatoes, diced

4 tbsp dry cider

450 g/1 lb green beans

2 tbsp snipped fresh chives, to garnish

salt and pepper

CINNAMON LAMB CASSEROLE

Season the flour with salt and pepper to taste then put it with the lamb in a polythene bag, hold the top closed and shake until the lamb cubes are lightly coated all over. Remove the lamb from the bag, shake off any excess flour and set aside.

Heat the oil in a large, flameproof casserole and cook the onions and garlic, stirring frequently, for 5 minutes, or until softened. Add the lamb and cook over a high heat, stirring frequently, for 5 minutes, or until browned on all sides and sealed.

Stir the wine, vinegar and tomatoes and their juice into the casserole, scraping any sediment from the base of the casserole, and bring to the boil. Reduce the heat and add the raisins, cinnamon, sugar and bay leaf. Season to taste with salt and pepper. Cover and simmer gently for 2 hours, or until the lamb is tender.

Meanwhile, make the topping. Put the yogurt into a small serving bowl, stir in the garlic and season to taste with salt and pepper. Cover and chill in the refrigerator until required.

Discard the bay leaf and serve hot, topped with a spoonful of the garlicky yogurt and dusted with paprika.

SERVES 6

- 2 tbsp plain flour
- 1 kg/2 lb 4 oz lean boneless lamb, cubed
- 2 tbsp olive oil
- 2 large onions, sliced
- 1 garlic clove, finely chopped
- 300 ml/10 fl oz full-bodied red wine
- 2 tbsp red wine vinegar
- 400 g/14 oz canned chopped tomatoes
- 55 g/2 oz seedless raisins
- 1 tbsp ground cinnamon
- pinch of sugar
- 1 bay leaf
- salt and pepper
- paprika, to garnish

topping
- 150 ml/5 fl oz natural Greek-style yogurt
- 2 garlic cloves, crushed
- salt and pepper

LAMB STEW WITH CHICKPEAS

SERVES 4–6

5 tbsp olive oil

225 g/8 oz chorizo sausage, cut into 5-mm/¼-inch thick slices, casings removed

2 large onions, chopped

6 large garlic cloves, crushed

900 g/2 lb boned leg of lamb, cut into 5-cm/2-inch chunks

250 ml/9 fl oz lamb stock or water

125 ml/4 fl oz red wine, such as Rioja or Tempranillo

2 tbsp sherry vinegar

800 g/1 lb 12 oz canned chopped tomatoes

4 sprigs fresh thyme, plus extra to garnish

2 bay leaves

½ tsp sweet Spanish paprika

800 g/1 lb 12 oz canned chickpeas, rinsed and drained

salt and pepper

Preheat the oven to 160°C/325°F/Gas Mark 4. Heat 4 tablespoons of the oil in a large, heavy-based flameproof casserole over a medium–high heat. Reduce the heat, add the chorizo and fry for 1 minute. Transfer to a plate. Add the onions to the casserole and fry for 2 minutes, then add the garlic and continue frying for 3 minutes, or until the onions are soft, but not brown. Remove from the casserole and set aside.

Heat the remaining 2 tablespoons of oil in the casserole. Add the lamb cubes in a single layer without over-crowding the casserole, and fry until browned on each side; work in batches, if necessary.

Return the onion mixture and chorizo to the casserole with all the lamb. Stir in the stock, wine, vinegar, tomatoes with their juices and salt and pepper to taste. Bring to the boil, scraping any glazed bits from the base of the casserole. Reduce the heat and stir in the thyme, bay leaves and paprika.

Transfer to the preheated oven and cook, covered, for 40–45 minutes until the lamb is tender. Stir in the chickpeas and return to the oven, uncovered, for 10 minutes, or until they are heated through and the juices are reduced.

Taste and adjust the seasoning. Serve garnished with thyme.

MEAT

123

SPICY LAMB & CHICKPEA STEW

Heat 1 tablespoon of the oil in a large saucepan or cast-iron casserole over a medium-high heat. Add the lamb, in batches if necessary to avoid crowding the pan, and cook until evenly browned on all sides, adding a little more oil if needed. Remove the meat with a slotted spoon when browned.

Reduce the heat and add the onion and garlic to the pan. Cook, stirring frequently, for 1–2 minutes.

Add the water and return all the meat to the pan. Bring just to the boil and skim off any scum that rises to the surface. Reduce the heat and stir in the tomatoes, bay leaf, thyme, oregano, cinnamon, cumin, turmeric and harissa. Simmer for about 1 hour, or until the meat is very tender. Discard the bay leaf.

Stir in the chickpeas, carrot and potato and simmer for 15 minutes. Add the courgette and peas and continue simmering for 15–20 minutes, or until all the vegetables are tender.

Taste and add more harissa, if desired. Ladle the soup into warmed bowls and garnish with mint or coriander.

SERVES 4–6

- 1–2 tbsp olive oil
- 450 g/1 lb boneless lamb, cut into cubes
- 1 onion, finely chopped
- 2–3 garlic cloves, crushed
- 1.2 litres/2 pints water
- 400 g/14 oz canned chopped tomatoes
- 1 bay leaf
- ½ tsp each thyme and oregano
- ⅛ tsp ground cinnamon
- ¼ tsp each cumin and turmeric
- 1 tsp harissa, or more to taste
- 400 g/14 oz canned chickpeas, rinsed and drained
- 1 carrot, diced
- 1 potato, diced
- 1 courgette, quartered lengthways and sliced
- 100 g/3½ oz fresh or defrosted frozen green peas
- sprigs of fresh mint or coriander, to garnish

IRISH STEW

Preheat the oven to 160°C/325°F/Gas Mark 3. Spread the flour on a plate and season with salt and pepper. Roll the pieces of lamb in the flour to coat, shaking off any excess, and arrange in the base of a casserole.

Layer the onions, carrots and potatoes on top of the lamb.

Sprinkle in the thyme and pour in the stock, then cover and cook in the preheated oven for 2½ hours. Garnish with the chopped fresh parsley and serve straight from the casserole.

SERVES 4

4 tbsp plain flour

1.3 kg/3 lb middle neck of lamb, trimmed of visible fat

3 large onions, chopped

3 carrots, sliced

450 g/1 lb potatoes, quartered

½ tsp dried thyme

850 ml/1½ pints hot beef stock

salt and pepper

2 tbsp chopped fresh parsley, to garnish

LAMB SHANKS

SERVES 6

- 1 tsp coriander seeds
- 1 tsp cumin seeds
- 1 tsp ground cinnamon
- 1 fresh green chilli, deseeded and finely chopped
- 1 garlic bulb, separated into cloves
- 125 ml/4 fl oz groundnut or sunflower oil
- grated rind of 1 lime
- 6 lamb shanks
- 2 onions, chopped
- 2 carrots, chopped
- 2 celery sticks, chopped
- 1 lime, chopped
- about 700 ml/1¼ pints beef stock or water
- 1 tsp sun-dried tomato purée
- 2 fresh mint sprigs
- 2 fresh rosemary sprigs, plus extra to garnish
- salt and pepper

Dry-fry the coriander and cumin seeds until fragrant, then pound with the cinnamon, chilli and 2 garlic cloves in a mortar and pestle. Stir in half the oil and the lime rind. Rub the spice paste all over the lamb and marinate for 4 hours.

Preheat the oven to 200°C/400°F/Gas Mark 6. Heat the remaining oil in a flameproof casserole and cook the lamb, turning frequently, until evenly browned. Chop the remaining garlic and add to the casserole with the onions, carrots, celery and lime, then pour in enough stock or water to cover. Stir in the tomato purée, add the herbs and season with salt and pepper.

Cover and cook in the preheated oven for 30 minutes. Reduce the oven temperature to 160°C/325°F/Gas Mark 3 and cook for a further 3 hours, or until very tender.

Transfer the lamb to a dish. Strain the cooking liquid to remove any solids, then return the liquid to the casserole. Boil until reduced and thickened. Serve the lamb with the sauce poured over it, garnished with sprigs of rosemary.

HEARTY WINTER BROTH

Heat the vegetable oil in a large, heavy-based saucepan and add the pieces of lamb, turning them to seal and brown on both sides. Lift the lamb out of the pan and set aside until required.

Add the onion, carrots and leeks to the saucepan and cook gently for about 3 minutes.

Return the lamb to the saucepan and add the vegetable stock, bay leaf, parsley and pearl barley to the saucepan. Bring the mixture in the pan to the boil, then reduce the heat. Cover and simmer for 1½ –2 hours.

Discard the parsley sprigs. Lift the pieces of lamb from the broth and allow them to cool slightly. Remove the bones and any fat and chop the meat. Return the lamb to the broth and reheat gently. Season to taste with salt and pepper.

It is advisable to prepare this soup a day ahead, then leave it to cool, cover and refrigerate overnight. When ready to serve, remove and discard the layer of fat from the surface and reheat the soup gently. Ladle into warmed bowls and serve immediately.

SERVES 4

1 tbsp vegetable oil

500 g/1 lb 2 oz lean neck of lamb

1 large onion, sliced

2 carrots, sliced

2 leeks, sliced

1 litre/1¾ pints vegetable stock

1 bay leaf

sprigs of fresh parsley

55 g/2 oz pearl barley

salt and pepper

OSSO BUCCO

Heat the oil and butter in a large, heavy-based frying pan. Add the onions and leek and cook over a low heat, stirring occasionally, for 5 minutes, until softened.

Spread out the flour on a plate and season with salt and pepper. Toss the pieces of veal in the flour to coat, shaking off any excess. Add the veal to the frying pan, increase the heat to high and cook until browned on both sides.

Gradually stir in the wine and stock and bring just to the boil, stirring constantly. Lower the heat, cover and simmer for 1¼ hours, or until the veal is very tender.

Meanwhile, make the gremolata by mixing the parsley, garlic and lemon rind in a small bowl.

Transfer the veal to a warmed serving dish with a slotted spoon. Bring the sauce to the boil and cook, stirring occasionally, until thickened and reduced. Pour the sauce over the veal, sprinkle with the gremolata and serve immediately.

SERVES 4

- 1 tbsp virgin olive oil
- 4 tbsp butter
- 2 onions, chopped
- 1 leek, sliced
- 3 tbsp plain flour
- 4 thick slices of veal shin (osso bucco)
- 300 ml/½ pint white wine
- 300 ml/½ pint veal or chicken stock
- salt and pepper

gremolata

- 2 tbsp chopped fresh parsley
- 1 garlic clove, finely chopped
- grated rind of 1 lemon

POULTRY

ITALIAN-STYLE ROAST CHICKEN

Preheat the oven to 190°C/375°F/Gas Mark 5. Rinse the chicken inside and out with cold water and drain well. Carefully cut between the skin and the top of the breast meat using a small pointed knife. Slide a finger into the slit and carefully enlarge it to form a pocket. Continue until the skin is completely lifted away from both breasts and the tops of the legs.

Chop the leaves from 3 rosemary stems. Mix with the feta cheese, sun-dried tomato purée, butter, and pepper to taste, then spoon under the skin. Put the chicken in a large roasting tin, cover with foil and cook in the preheated oven, calculating the cooking time as 20 minutes per 500 g/1 lb 2 oz, plus 20 minutes.

Break the garlic bulb into cloves but do not peel. Add the vegetables and garlic to the roasting tin. After 40 minutes, drizzle with oil, tuck in a few stems of rosemary and season with salt and pepper. Cook for the remaining calculated time, removing the foil for the last 40 minutes to brown the chicken.

Transfer the chicken to a serving platter. Place some of the vegetables around the chicken and transfer the remainder to a warmed serving dish. Spoon the fat out of the roasting tin (it will be floating on top) and stir the flour into the remaining cooking juices. Place the roasting tin on top of the hob and cook over a medium heat for 2 minutes, then gradually stir in the stock. Bring to the boil, stirring until thickened and season to taste. Strain into a gravy boat and serve with the chicken.

SERVES 6

2.5 kg/5 lb 8 oz chicken

fresh rosemary sprigs

175 g/6 oz feta cheese, coarsely grated

2 tbsp sun-dried tomato purée

60 g/2 oz butter, softened

1 bulb garlic

1 kg/2 lb 4 oz new potatoes, halved if large

1 each red, green and yellow pepper, deseeded and cut into chunks

3 courgettes, thinly sliced

2 tbsp olive oil

2 tbsp plain flour

600 ml/1 pint chicken stock

salt and pepper

CHICKEN IN WHITE WINE

Preheat the oven to 160°C/325°F/Gas Mark 3. Melt half the butter with the oil in a flameproof casserole. Add the bacon and cook over a medium heat, stirring, for 5–10 minutes, or until golden brown. Transfer the bacon to a large plate. Add the onions and garlic to the casserole and cook over a low heat, stirring occasionally, for 10 minutes, or until golden. Transfer to the plate. Add the chicken and cook over a medium heat, stirring constantly, for 8–10 minutes, or until golden. Transfer to the plate.

Drain off any excess fat from the casserole. Stir in the wine and stock and bring to the boil, scraping any sediment off the base. Add the bouquet garni and season to taste. Return the bacon, onions and chicken to the casserole. Cover and cook in the preheated oven for 1 hour. Add the mushrooms, re-cover and cook for 15 minutes. Meanwhile, make a beurre manié by mashing the remaining butter with the flour in a small bowl.

Remove the casserole from the oven and set over a medium heat. Remove and discard the bouquet garni. Whisk in the beurre manié, a little at a time. Bring to the boil, stirring constantly, then serve, garnished with fresh herbs.

SERVES 4

55 g/2 oz butter

2 tbsp olive oil

2 rindless, thick streaky bacon rashers, chopped

115 g/4 oz baby onions, peeled

1 garlic clove, finely chopped

1.8 kg/4 lb chicken pieces

400 ml/14 fl oz dry white wine

300 ml/10 fl oz chicken stock

1 bouquet garni

115 g/4 oz button mushrooms

25 g/1 oz plain flour

salt and pepper

fresh mixed herbs, to garnish

COQ AU VIN

55 g/2 oz butter

1 tbsp olive oil

1.8 kg/4 lb chicken pieces

115 g/4 oz rindless smoked bacon, cut into strips

115 g/4 oz baby onions

115 g/4 oz chestnut mushrooms, halved

2 garlic cloves, finely chopped

3 tbsp brandy

225 ml/8 fl oz red wine

300 ml/10 fl oz chicken stock

1 bouquet garni

2 tbsp plain flour

salt and pepper

bay leaves, to garnish

Melt half the butter with the olive oil in a large, flameproof casserole. Add the chicken and cook over a medium heat, stirring, for 8–10 minutes, or until golden brown all over. Add the bacon, onions, mushrooms and garlic.

Pour in the brandy and set it alight with a match or taper. When the flames have died down, add the wine, stock and bouquet garni and season to taste with salt and pepper. Bring to the boil, reduce the heat and simmer gently for 1 hour, or until the chicken pieces are cooked through and tender. Meanwhile, make a beurre manié by mashing the remaining butter with the flour in a small bowl.

Remove and discard the bouquet garni. Transfer the chicken to a large plate and keep warm. Stir the beurre manié into the casserole, a little at a time. Bring to the boil, return the chicken to the casserole and serve immediately, garnished with bay leaves.

POULTRY

141

SPICED CHICKEN STEW

POULTRY

142

Season the chicken pieces with salt and dust with paprika.

Heat the oil and butter in a flameproof casserole or large saucepan. Add the chicken pieces and cook over a medium heat, turning, for 10–15 minutes, or until golden. Transfer to a plate with a slotted spoon.

Add the onion and peppers to the casserole. Cook over a low heat, stirring occasionally, for 5 minutes, or until softened. Add the tomatoes, wine, stock, Worcestershire sauce, Tabasco sauce and parsley and bring to the boil, stirring. Return the chicken to the casserole, cover and simmer, stirring occasionally, for 30 minutes.

Add the sweetcorn and beans to the casserole, partially re-cover and simmer for a further 30 minutes. Place the flour and water in a small bowl and mix to make a paste. Stir a ladleful of the cooking liquid into the paste, then stir it into the stew. Cook, stirring frequently, for 5 minutes. Serve, garnished with parsley.

SERVES 6

1.8 kg/4 lb chicken pieces

2 tbsp paprika

2 tbsp olive oil

25 g/1 oz butter

450 g/1 lb onions, chopped

2 yellow peppers, deseeded and chopped

400 g/14 oz canned chopped tomatoes

225 ml/8 fl oz dry white wine

450 ml/16 fl oz chicken stock

1 tbsp Worcestershire sauce

½ tsp Tabasco

1 tbsp finely chopped fresh parsley

325 g/11½ oz canned sweetcorn kernels, drained

425 g/15 oz canned butter beans, drained and rinsed

2 tbsp plain flour

4 tbsp water

salt

fresh parsley sprigs, to garnish

HUNTER'S CHICKEN

Preheat the oven to 160°C/325°F/Gas Mark 3. Heat the butter and oil in a flameproof casserole and cook the chicken over a medium–high heat, turning frequently, for 10 minutes, or until golden all over and sealed. Using a slotted spoon, transfer to a plate.

Add the onions and garlic to the casserole and cook over a low heat, stirring occasionally, for 10 minutes, or until softened and golden. Add the tomatoes with their juice, the herbs, sun-dried tomato purée and wine, and season to taste with salt and pepper. Bring to the boil, then return the chicken portions to the casserole, pushing them down into the sauce.

Cover and cook in the preheated oven for 50 minutes. Add the mushrooms and cook for a further 10 minutes, or until the chicken is tender and the juices run clear when a skewer is inserted into the thickest part of the meat. Serve immediately.

SERVES 4

15 g/½ oz unsalted butter

2 tbsp olive oil

1.8 kg/4 lb skinned chicken portions

2 red onions, sliced

2 garlic cloves, finely chopped

400 g/14 oz canned chopped tomatoes

2 tbsp chopped fresh flat-leaf parsley

6 fresh basil leaves, torn

1 tbsp sun-dried tomato purée

150 ml/5 fl oz red wine

225 g/8 oz mushrooms, sliced

salt and pepper

FLORIDA
CHICKEN

SERVES 4

450 g/1 lb skinless, boneless chicken

1½ tbsp plain flour

1 tbsp olive oil

1 onion, cut into wedges

2 celery sticks, sliced

150 ml/5 fl oz orange juice

300 ml/10 fl oz chicken stock

1 tbsp light soy sauce

1-2 tsp clear honey

1 tbsp grated orange rind

1 orange pepper, deseeded and chopped

225 g/8 oz courgettes, sliced into half moons

1 small corn on the cob, halved, or 100 g/3½ oz baby sweetcorn

1 orange, peeled and segmented

salt and pepper

1 tbsp chopped fresh parsley, to garnish

Lightly rinse the chicken and pat dry with kitchen paper. Cut into bite-sized pieces. Season the flour well with salt and pepper. Toss the chicken in the seasoned flour until well coated and reserve any remaining seasoned flour.

Heat the oil in a large, heavy-based frying pan and cook the chicken over a high heat, stirring frequently, for 5 minutes, or until golden on all sides and sealed. Using a slotted spoon, transfer the chicken to a plate.

Add the onion and celery to the frying pan and cook over a medium heat, stirring frequently, for 5 minutes, or until softened. Sprinkle in the reserved seasoned flour and cook, stirring constantly, for 2 minutes, then remove from the heat. Gradually stir in the orange juice, stock, soy sauce and honey, followed by the orange rind, then return to the heat and bring to the boil, stirring.

Return the chicken to the frying pan. Reduce the heat, cover and simmer, stirring occasionally, for 15 minutes. Add the orange pepper, courgettes and corn on the cob and simmer for a further 10 minutes, or until the chicken and vegetables are tender. Add the orange segments, stir well and heat through for 1 minute. Serve garnished with the parsley.

CHICKEN & BARLEY STEW

Heat the oil in a large saucepan over a medium heat. Add the chicken and cook for 3 minutes, then turn over and cook on the other side for a further 2 minutes. Add the stock, barley, potatoes, carrots, leek, shallots, tomato purée and bay leaf. Bring to the boil, lower the heat and simmer for 30 minutes.

Add the courgette and chopped parsley, cover the pan and cook for a further 20 minutes, or until the chicken is cooked through. Remove the bay leaf and discard.

In a separate bowl, mix the flour with 4 tablespoons of water and stir into a smooth paste. Add it to the stew and cook, stirring, over a low heat for a further 5 minutes. Season to taste with salt and pepper.

Remove from the heat, ladle into individual serving bowls and garnish with sprigs of fresh parsley.

SERVES 4

2 tbsp vegetable oil

8 small, skinless chicken thighs

500 ml/18 fl oz chicken stock

100 g/3½ oz pearl barley, rinsed
  and drained

200 g/7 oz small new potatoes,
  scrubbed and halved lengthways

2 large carrots, peeled and sliced

1 leek, trimmed and sliced

2 shallots, sliced

1 tbsp tomato purée

1 bay leaf

1 courgette, trimmed and sliced

2 tbsp chopped fresh flat-leaf
  parsley, plus extra sprigs
  to garnish

2 tbsp plain flour

4 tbsp water

salt and pepper

CHICKEN WITH GARLIC

Sift the flour onto a large plate and season with paprika and salt and pepper to taste. Coat the chicken pieces with the flour on both sides, shaking off the excess.

Heat 4 tablespoons of the oil in a large, deep frying pan or flameproof casserole over a medium heat. Add the garlic and fry, stirring frequently, for about 2 minutes to flavour the oil. Remove the garlic with a slotted spoon and set aside to drain on kitchen paper.

Working in batches, add the chicken pieces to the pan, skin-side down, adding a little extra oil if necessary. Fry for 5 minutes until the skin is golden brown. Turn over and fry for 5 minutes more, then transfer to a plate.

Pour off any excess oil. Return the garlic and chicken pieces to the pan and add the stock, wine and herbs. Bring to the boil, then reduce the heat, cover and simmer for 20–25 minutes until the chicken is cooked through and tender and the garlic is very soft.

Transfer the chicken pieces to a serving platter and keep warm. Bring the cooking liquid to the boil, with the garlic and herbs, and boil until reduced to about 300 ml/½ pint. Remove and discard the cooked herbs. Taste and adjust the seasoning, if necessary.

Spoon the sauce and the garlic cloves over the chicken pieces. Garnish with fresh parsley and thyme, and serve.

SERVES 6

4 tbsp plain flour

Spanish paprika, either hot or smoked sweet, to taste

1 large chicken, about 1.75 kg/ 3 lb 12 oz, cut into 8 pieces, rinsed and patted dry

4–6 tbsp olive oil

24 large garlic cloves, peeled and halved

450 ml/¾ pint chicken stock

4 tbsp dry white wine, such as white Rioja

2 sprigs of fresh flat-leaf parsley, 1 bay leaf and 1 sprig of fresh thyme, tied together

salt and pepper

fresh flat-leaf parsley and thyme leaves, to garnish

CHICKEN RISOTTO WITH SAFFRON

SERVES 4

125 g/4½ oz butter

900 g/2 lb skinless, boneless chicken breasts, thinly sliced

1 large onion, chopped

500 g/1 lb 2 oz risotto rice

150 ml/5 fl oz white wine

1 tsp crumbled saffron threads

1.3 litres/2¼ pints chicken stock

55 g/2 oz freshly grated Parmesan cheese

salt and pepper

Heat 55 g/2 oz of the butter in a deep saucepan. Add the chicken and onion and cook, stirring frequently, for 8 minutes, or until golden brown.

Add the rice and mix to coat in the butter. Cook, stirring constantly for 2–3 minutes, or until the grains are translucent. Add the wine and cook, stirring constantly, for 1 minute until reduced.

Mix the saffron with 4 tablespoons of the hot stock. Add to the rice and cook, stirring constantly, until it is absorbed.

Gradually add the remaining hot stock, a ladle at a time. Stir constantly and add more liquid as the rice absorbs each addition. Cook for 20 minutes, or until all the liquid is absorbed and the rice is creamy. Season to taste.

Remove the risotto from the heat and add the remaining butter. Mix well, then stir in the Parmesan until it melts. Spoon the risotto onto warmed plates and serve immediately.

PAPPARDELLE WITH CHICKEN & PORCINI

Place the porcini in a small bowl, add the hot water and leave to soak for 20 minutes. Meanwhile, place the tomatoes and their can juices in a heavy-based saucepan and break them up with a wooden spoon, then stir in the chilli. Bring to the boil, reduce the heat and simmer, stirring occasionally, for 30 minutes, or until reduced.

Remove the mushrooms from their soaking liquid with a perforated spoon, reserving the liquid. Sieve the liquid through a coffee filter paper or muslin-lined sieve into the tomatoes and simmer for a further 15 minutes.

Meanwhile, heat 2 tablespoons of the olive oil in a heavy-based frying pan. Add the chicken and cook, stirring frequently, until golden brown all over and tender. Stir in the mushrooms and garlic and cook for a further 5 minutes.

While the chicken is cooking, bring a large, heavy-based saucepan of lightly salted water to the boil. Add the pasta, return to the boil and cook for 8–10 minutes, or until tender but still firm to the bite. Drain well, transfer to a warmed serving dish, drizzle with the remaining olive oil and toss lightly. Stir in the chicken mixture into the tomato sauce, season to taste with salt and pepper and spoon on top of the pasta. Toss lightly, sprinkle with parsley and serve immediately.

SERVES 4

- 40 g/1½ oz dried porcini mushrooms
- 175 ml/6 fl oz hot water
- 800 g/1 lb 12 oz canned chopped tomatoes
- 1 fresh red chilli, deseeded and finely chopped
- 3 tbsp olive oil
- 350 g/12 oz skinless, boneless chicken, cut into thin strips
- 2 garlic cloves, finely chopped
- 350 g/12 oz dried pappardelle
- salt and pepper
- 2 tbsp chopped fresh flat-leaf parsley, to garnish

CHICKEN PEPPERONATA

Toss the chicken thighs in the flour, shaking off the excess.

Heat the oil in a wide frying pan and fry the chicken quickly until sealed and lightly browned, then remove the chicken from the pan.

Add the onion to the pan and gently fry until soft. Add the garlic, peppers, tomatoes and oregano, then bring to the boil, stirring.

Arrange the chicken over the vegetables, season well with salt and pepper, then cover the pan tightly and simmer for 20–25 minutes or until the chicken is completely cooked and tender.

Taste and adjust the seasoning if necessary, garnish with oregano and serve with crusty wholemeal bread.

SERVES 4

8 skinless chicken thighs

2 tbsp wholemeal flour

2 tbsp olive oil

1 small onion, thinly sliced

1 garlic clove, crushed

1 each large red, yellow and green peppers, deseeded and thinly sliced

400 g/14 oz canned chopped tomatoes

1 tbsp chopped oregano, plus extra to garnish

salt and pepper

crusty wholemeal bread, to serve

LOUISIANA CHICKEN

SERVES 4

tbsp sunflower oil

chicken portions

5 g/2 oz plain flour

onion, chopped

celery sticks, sliced

green pepper, deseeded and chopped

garlic cloves, finely chopped

tsp chopped fresh thyme

fresh red chillies, deseeded and finely chopped

oo g/14 oz canned chopped tomatoes

oo ml/10 fl oz chicken stock

alt and pepper

mb's lettuce and chopped fresh thyme, to garnish

Heat the oil in a large, heavy-based saucepan or flameproof casserole. Add the chicken and cook over a medium heat, stirring, for 5–10 minutes, or until golden. Transfer the chicken to a plate with a slotted spoon.

Stir the flour into the oil and cook over a very low heat, stirring constantly, for 15 minutes, or until light golden. Do not let it burn. Add the onion, celery and green pepper and cook, stirring constantly, for 2 minutes. Add the garlic, thyme and chillies and cook, stirring, for 1 minute.

Stir in the tomatoes and their juices, then gradually stir in the stock. Return the chicken pieces to the saucepan, cover and simmer for 45 minutes, or until the chicken is cooked through and tender. Season to taste with salt and pepper, transfer to warmed serving plates and serve immediately, garnished with some lettuce leaves and a sprinkling of chopped thyme.

CHICKEN TAGINE

Heat the oil in a large saucepan over a medium heat, add the onion and garlic and cook for 3 minutes, stirring frequently. Add the chicken and cook, stirring constantly, for a further 5 minutes, or until sealed on all sides. Add the cumin and cinnamon sticks to the saucepan halfway through sealing the chicken.

Sprinkle in the flour and cook, stirring constantly, for 2 minutes. Add the aubergine, red pepper and mushrooms and cook for a further 2 minutes, stirring constantly.

Blend the tomato purée with the stock, stir into the saucepan and bring to the boil. Reduce the heat and add the chickpeas and apricots. Cover and simmer for 15–20 minutes, or until the chicken is tender.

Season with salt and pepper to taste and serve immediately, sprinkled with coriander.

SERVES 4

1 tbsp olive oil

1 onion, cut into small wedges

2–4 garlic cloves, sliced

450 g/1 lb skinless, boneless chicken breast, diced

1 tsp ground cumin

2 cinnamon sticks, lightly bruised

1 tbsp plain wholemeal flour

225 g/8 oz aubergine, diced

1 red pepper, deseeded and chopped

85 g/3 oz button mushrooms, sliced

1 tbsp tomato purée

600 ml/1 pint chicken stock

280 g/10 oz canned chickpeas, drained and rinsed

55 g/2 oz ready-to-eat dried apricots, chopped

salt and pepper

1 tbsp chopped fresh coriander, to garnish

BALTI CHICKEN

Heat the ghee in a large, heavy-based frying pan. Add the onions and cook over a low heat, stirring occasionally, for 10 minutes, or until golden. Add the sliced tomatoes, kalonji seeds, peppercorns, cardamom pods, cinnamon stick, chilli powder, garam masala, garlic purée and ginger purée, and season with salt to taste. Cook, stirring constantly, for 5 minutes.

Add the chicken and cook, stirring constantly, for 5 minutes, or until well coated in the spice paste. Stir in the yogurt. Cover and simmer, stirring occasionally, for 10 minutes.

Stir in the chopped coriander, chillies and lime juice. Transfer to a warmed serving dish, sprinkle with more chopped coriander and serve immediately.

SERVES 6

3 tbsp ghee or vegetable oil

2 large onions, sliced

3 tomatoes, sliced

½ tsp kalonji seeds

4 black peppercorns

2 cardamom pods

1 cinnamon stick

1 tsp chilli powder

1 tsp garam masala

1 tsp garlic purée

1 tsp ginger purée

700 g/1 lb 9 oz skinless, boneless chicken breasts or thighs, diced

2 tbsp natural yogurt

2 tbsp chopped fresh coriander, plus extra to garnish

2 fresh green chillies, deseeded and finely chopped

2 tbsp lime juice

salt

SPICY AROMATIC CHICKEN

- 4–8 chicken pieces, skinned
- 1/2 lemon, cut into wedges
- 4 tbsp olive oil
- 1 onion, roughly chopped
- 2 large garlic cloves, finely chopped
- 125 ml/4 fl oz dry white wine
- 400 g/14 oz canned chopped tomatoes in juice
- pinch of sugar
- 1/2 tsp ground cinnamon
- 1/2 tsp ground cloves
- 1/2 tsp ground allspice
- 400g/14 oz canned artichoke hearts or okra, drained
- 8 black olives, stoned
- salt and pepper

Rub the chicken pieces with the lemon. Heat the oil in a large flameproof casserole or lidded frying pan. Add the onion and garlic and fry for 5 minutes, until softened. Add the chicken pieces and fry for 5–10 minutes, until browned on all sides.

Pour in the wine and add the tomatoes with their juice, the sugar, cinnamon, cloves, allspice, and salt and pepper and bring to the boil. Cover the casserole and simmer for 45 minutes–1 hour, until the chicken is tender.

Meanwhile, cut the artichoke hearts in half. Add the artichokes and the olives to the casserole 10 minutes before the end of cooking, and continue to simmer until heated through. Serve hot.

POULTRY

165

THAI GREEN CHICKEN CURRY

Heat 2 tablespoons of oil in a preheated wok or large, heavy-based frying pan. Add 2 tablespoons of the curry paste and stir-fry briefly until all the aromas are released.

Add the chicken, lime leaves and lemon grass and stir-fry for 3–4 minutes, until the meat is beginning to colour. Add the coconut milk and aubergines and simmer gently for 8–10 minutes, or until tender.

Stir in the fish sauce and serve immediately, garnished with Thai basil sprigs and lime leaves.

SERVES 4

2 tbsp groundnut or sunflower oil

2 tbsp ready-made Thai green curry paste

500 g/1 lb 2 oz skinless boneless chicken breasts, cut into cubes

2 kaffir lime leaves, roughly torn

1 lemon grass stalk, finely chopped

225 ml/8 fl oz canned coconut milk

16 baby aubergines, halved

2 tbsp Thai fish sauce

fresh Thai basil sprigs and kaffir lime leaves, thinly sliced, to garnish

CHICKEN
JALFREZI

Grind the cumin and coriander seeds in a mortar with a pestle, then reserve. Heat the mustard oil in a large, heavy-based frying pan over a high heat for 1 minute, or until it begins to smoke. Add the vegetable oil, reduce the heat and add the onion and garlic. Cook for 10 minutes, or until golden.

Add the tomato purée, chopped tomatoes, turmeric, ground cumin and coriander seeds, chilli powder, garam masala and vinegar to the frying pan. Stir the mixture until fragrant.

Add the red pepper and broad beans and stir for a further 2 minutes, or until the pepper is softened. Stir in the chicken, and season to taste with salt. Simmer gently for 6–8 minutes, or until the chicken is heated through and the beans are tender. Transfer to warmed serving bowls, garnish with coriander sprigs and serve with freshly cooked rice.

SERVES 4

½ tsp cumin seeds

½ tsp coriander seeds

1 tsp mustard oil

3 tbsp vegetable oil

1 large onion, finely chopped

3 garlic cloves, crushed

1 tbsp tomato purée

2 tomatoes, peeled and chopped

1 tsp ground turmeric

½ tsp chilli powder

½ tsp garam masala

1 tsp red wine vinegar

1 small red pepper, deseeded and chopped

125 g/4½ oz frozen broad beans

500 g/1 lb 2 oz cooked chicken, chopped

salt

fresh coriander sprigs, to garnish

freshly cooked rice, to serve

JAMBALAYA

SERVES 4

2 tbsp vegetable oil

2 onions, roughly chopped

1 green pepper, deseeded and
roughly chopped

2 celery sticks, roughly chopped

3 garlic cloves, finely chopped

2 tsp paprika

300 g/1½ oz skinless, boneless
chicken breasts, chopped

400 g/3½ oz kabanos sausages,
chopped

3 tomatoes, peeled and chopped

450 g/1 lb long-grain rice

350 ml/1½ pints hot chicken or
fish stock

1 tsp dried oregano

2 bay leaves

12 large raw prawns

4 spring onions, finely chopped

2 tbsp chopped fresh parsley

salt and pepper

chopped fresh herbs, to garnish

Heat the vegetable oil in a large frying pan over a low heat. Add the onions, pepper, celery and garlic and cook for 8–10 minutes until all the vegetables have softened. Add the paprika and cook for a further 30 seconds. Add the chicken and sausages and cook for 8–10 minutes until lightly browned. Add the tomatoes and cook for 2–3 minutes until they have collapsed.

Add the rice to the pan and stir well. Pour in the hot stock, oregano and bay leaves and stir well. Cover and simmer for 10 minutes.

Add the prawns and stir. Cover again and cook for a further 6–8 minutes until the rice is tender and the prawns are cooked through.

Stir in the spring onions and parsley and season to taste with salt and pepper. Transfer to a large serving dish, garnish with chopped fresh herbs and serve.

ITALIAN TURKEY CUTLETS

Preheat the grill to medium. Heat the oil in a flameproof casserole or heavy-based frying pan. Add the turkey escalopes and cook over a medium heat for 5–10 minutes, turning occasionally, until golden. Transfer to a plate.

Add the red pepper and onion to the frying pan and cook over a low heat, stirring occasionally, for 5 minutes, or until softened. Add the garlic and cook for a further 2 minutes.

Return the turkey to the frying pan and add the passata, wine and marjoram. Season to taste with salt and pepper. Bring to the boil, then reduce the heat, cover and simmer, stirring occasionally, for 25–30 minutes, or until the turkey is cooked through and tender.

Stir in the cannellini beans and simmer for a further 5 minutes. Sprinkle the breadcrumbs over the top and place under the preheated grill for 2–3 minutes, or until golden. Serve, garnished with fresh basil sprigs.

1 tbsp olive oil

4 turkey escalopes or steaks

2 red peppers, deseeded and sliced

1 red onion, sliced

2 garlic cloves, finely chopped

300 ml/10 fl oz passata

150 ml/5 fl oz medium white wine

1 tbsp chopped fresh marjoram

400 g/14 oz canned cannellini beans, drained and rinsed

3 tbsp fresh white breadcrumbs

salt and pepper

fresh basil sprigs, to garnish

MEXICAN TURKEY

Preheat the oven to 160°C/325°F/Gas Mark 3. Spread the flour on a plate and season with salt and pepper. Coat the turkey fillets in the seasoned flour, shaking off any excess. Reserve any remaining seasoned flour.

Heat the oil in a flameproof casserole. Add the turkey fillets and cook over a medium heat, turning occasionally, for 5–10 minutes, or until golden. Transfer to a plate with a slotted spoon.

Add the onion and red pepper to the casserole. Cook over a low heat, stirring occasionally, for 5 minutes, or until softened. Sprinkle in the remaining seasoned flour and cook, stirring constantly, for 1 minute. Gradually stir in the stock, then add the raisins, chopped tomatoes, chilli powder, cinnamon, cumin and chocolate. Season to taste with salt and pepper. Bring to the boil, stirring constantly.

Return the turkey to the casserole, cover and cook in the preheated oven for 50 minutes. Serve immediately, garnished with sprigs of coriander.

SERVES 4

55 g/2 oz plain flour

4 turkey breast fillets

3 tbsp corn oil

1 onion, thinly sliced

1 red pepper, deseeded and sliced

300 ml/10 fl oz chicken stock

25 g/1 oz raisins

4 tomatoes, peeled, deseeded and chopped

1 tsp chilli powder

½ tsp ground cinnamon

pinch of ground cumin

25 g/1 oz plain chocolate, finely chopped or grated

salt and pepper

sprigs of fresh coriander, to garnish

DUCK LEGS
WITH OLIVES

duck legs, all visible fat
trimmed off

00 g/1 lb 12 oz canned tomatoes,
chopped

garlic cloves, peeled but
left whole

arge onion, chopped

carrot, finely chopped

celery stick, finely chopped

sprigs fresh thyme

0 g/3½ oz Spanish green olives
n brine, stuffed with pimientos,
garlic or almonds, drained
and rinsed

tsp finely grated orange rind

lt and pepper

Put the duck legs in the bottom of a flameproof casserole or a
large, heavy-based frying pan with a tight-fitting lid. Add the
tomatoes, garlic, onion, carrot, celery, thyme and olives and stir
together. Season to taste with salt and pepper.

Turn the heat to high and cook, uncovered, until the ingredients
begin to bubble. Reduce the heat to low, cover tightly and
simmer for 1¼–1½ hours until the duck is very tender. Check
occasionally and add a little water if the mixture appears to be
drying out.

When the duck is tender, transfer it to a serving platter, cover
and keep hot in a preheated warm oven. Leave the casserole
uncovered, increase the heat to medium and cook, stirring, for
about 10 minutes until the mixture forms a sauce. Stir in the
orange rind, then taste and adjust the seasoning if necessary.

Mash the tender garlic cloves with a fork and spread over the
duck legs. Spoon the sauce over the top. Serve at once.

DUCK JAMBALAYA-STYLE STEW

Remove and discard the skin and any fat from the duck breasts.
Cut the flesh into bite-sized pieces.

Heat half the oil in a large deep frying pan and cook the duck,
gammon and chorizo over a high heat, stirring frequently, for
5 minutes, or until browned on all sides and sealed. Using
a slotted spoon, remove from the frying pan and set aside.

Add the onion, garlic, celery and chillies to the frying pan and
cook over a medium heat, stirring frequently, for 5 minutes,
or until softened. Add the green pepper, then stir in the stock,
oregano, tomatoes and hot pepper sauce.

Bring to the boil, then reduce the heat and return the duck,
gammon and chorizo to the frying pan. Cover and simmer, stirring
occasionally, for 20 minutes, or until the duck and gammon
are tender.

Serve immediately, garnished with parsley and accompanied by
a green salad and rice.

SERVES 4

4 duck breasts, about
150 g/5½ oz each

2 tbsp olive oil

225 g/8 oz piece gammon, cut
into small chunks

225 g/8 oz chorizo, outer casing
removed

1 onion, chopped

3 garlic cloves, chopped

3 celery sticks, chopped

1–2 fresh red chillies, deseeded
and chopped

1 green pepper, deseeded and
chopped

600 ml/1 pint chicken stock

1 tbsp chopped fresh oregano

400 g/14 oz canned chopped
tomatoes

1–2 tsp hot pepper sauce, or
to taste

chopped fresh flat-leaf parsley,
to garnish

green salad and freshly cooked
rice, to serve

FISH & SEAFOOD

MONKFISH PARCELS

Preheat the oven to 190°C/375°F/Gas Mark 5. Cut 4 large pieces of foil, each about 23 cm/9 inches square. Brush them lightly with a little of the oil, then divide the courgettes and pepper among them.

Rinse the fish fillets under cold running water and pat dry with kitchen paper. Cut them in half, then put 1 piece on top of each pile of courgettes and pepper. Cut the bacon rashers in half and lay 3 pieces across each piece of fish. Season to taste with salt and pepper, drizzle over the remaining oil and close up the parcels. Seal tightly, transfer to an ovenproof dish and bake in the preheated oven for 25 minutes.

Remove from the oven, open each foil parcel slightly and serve with pasta and slices of olive bread.

SERVES 4

- 4 tsp olive oil
- 2 courgettes, sliced
- 1 large red pepper, peeled, deseeded and cut into strips
- 2 monkfish fillets, about 125 g/ 4½ oz each, skin and membrane removed
- 6 smoked streaky bacon rashers
- salt and pepper
- freshly cooked pasta and slices of olive bread, to serve

ROASTED
MONKFISH

Preheat the oven to 200°C/400°F/Gas Mark 6. Remove the central bone from the fish if not already removed and make small slits down each fillet. Cut 2 of the garlic cloves into thin slivers and insert into the fish. Place the fish on a sheet of greaseproof paper, season to taste with salt and pepper and drizzle over 1 tablespoon of the oil. Bring the top edges together. Form into a pleat and fold over, then fold the ends underneath, completely encasing the fish. Reserve.

Put the remaining garlic cloves and all the vegetables into a roasting tin and drizzle with the remaining oil, turning the vegetables so that they are well coated in the oil.

Roast in the preheated oven for 20 minutes, turning occasionally. Put the fish parcel on top of the vegetables and cook for a further 15–20 minutes, or until the vegetables are tender and the fish is cooked.

Remove from the oven and open up the parcel. Cut the monkfish into thick slices. Arrange the vegetables on warmed serving plates, top with the fish slices and sprinkle with the basil. Serve immediately.

SERVES 4

- 675 g/1 lb 8 oz monkfish tail, skinned
- 4–5 large garlic cloves, peeled
- 3 tbsp olive oil
- 1 onion, cut into wedges
- 1 small aubergine, about 300 g/10½ oz, cut into chunks
- 1 red pepper, deseeded, cut into wedges
- 1 yellow pepper, deseeded, cut into wedges
- 1 large courgette, about 225 g/8 oz, cut into wedges
- salt and pepper
- 1 tbsp shredded fresh basil, to garnish

MEDITERRANEAN SWORDFISH

SERVES 4

tbsp olive oil

onion, finely chopped

celery stick, finely chopped

115 g/4 oz green olives, stoned

450 g/1 lb tomatoes, chopped

tbsp bottled capers, drained

swordfish steaks, about
140 g/5 oz each

alt and pepper

resh flat-leaf parsley sprigs,
to garnish

Heat the oil in a large, heavy-based frying pan. Add the onion and
celery and cook over a low heat, stirring occasionally, for
5 minutes, or until softened.

Meanwhile, roughly chop half the olives. Stir the chopped and
whole olives into the saucepan with the tomatoes and capers and
season to taste with salt and pepper.

Bring to the boil, then reduce the heat, cover and simmer
gently, stirring occasionally, for 15 minutes.

Add the swordfish steaks to the frying pan and return to the
boil. Cover and simmer, turning the fish once, for 20 minutes, or
until the fish is cooked and the flesh flakes easily. Transfer the
fish to serving plates and spoon the sauce over them. Garnish
with fresh parsley sprigs and serve immediately.

FISH & SEAFOOD

SICILIAN TUNA

Whisk all the marinade ingredients together in a small bowl. Put the tuna steaks in a large, shallow dish and spoon over 4 tablespoons of the marinade, turning until well coated. Cover and leave to marinate in the refrigerator for 30 minutes. Reserve the remaining marinade.

Heat a ridged pan over a high heat. Put the fennel and onions in a separate bowl, add the oil and toss well to coat. Add to the pan and cook for 5 minutes on each side until just beginning to colour. Transfer to 4 warmed serving plates, drizzle with the reserved marinade and keep warm.

Add the tuna steaks to the pan and cook, turning once, for 4–5 minutes until firm to the touch but still moist inside. Transfer the tuna to the serving plates and serve immediately with crusty rolls.

SERVES 4

4 tuna steaks, about 140 g/5 oz each

2 fennel bulbs, thickly sliced lengthways

2 red onions, sliced

2 tbsp extra virgin olive oil

crusty rolls, to serve

marinade

125 ml/4 fl oz extra virgin olive oil

4 garlic cloves, finely chopped

4 fresh red chillies, deseeded and finely chopped

juice and finely grated rind of 2 lemons

4 tbsp finely chopped fresh flat-leaf parsley

salt and pepper

FISH STEW
WITH CIDER

Melt the butter in a large saucepan over a medium–low heat.
Add the leek and shallots and cook for about 5 minutes, stirring
frequently, until they start to soften. Add the cider and bring
to the boil.

Stir in the stock, potatoes and bay leaf with a large pinch of
salt (unless the stock is salty) and bring back to the boil. Reduce
the heat, cover and cook gently for 10 minutes.

Put the flour in a small bowl and very slowly whisk in a few
tablespoons of the milk to make a thick paste. Stir in a little more
to make a smooth liquid.

Adjust the heat so the stew bubbles gently. Stir in the flour
mixture and cook, stirring frequently, for 5 minutes. Add the
remaining milk and half the cream. Continue cooking for about
10 minutes until the potatoes are tender.

Chop the sorrel finely and combine with the remaining cream.
Stir the sorrel cream into the stew and add the fish. Continue
cooking, stirring occasionally, for about 3 minutes, until the
monkfish stiffens. Taste the stew and adjust the seasoning, if
needed. Ladle into warmed bowls and serve.

SERVES 4

2 tsp butter

1 large leek, thinly sliced

2 shallots, finely chopped

125 ml/4 fl oz dry cider

300 ml/10 fl oz fish stock

250 g/9 oz potatoes, diced

1 bay leaf

4 tbsp plain flour

200 ml/7 fl oz milk

200 ml/7 fl oz double cream

55 g/2 oz fresh sorrel leaves

350 g/12 oz skinless monkfish or
   cod fillet, cut into 2.5-cm/1-inch
   pieces

salt and pepper

CATALAN FISH STEW

SERVES 4–6

large pinch of saffron threads

4 tbsp almost-boiling water

5 tbsp olive oil

1 large onion, chopped

2 garlic cloves, finely chopped

1½ tbsp chopped fresh thyme
leaves

2 bay leaves

2 red peppers, deseeded and
roughly chopped

800 g/1 lb 12 oz canned chopped
tomatoes

1 tsp smoked paprika

250 ml/9 fl oz fish stock

140 g/5 oz blanched almonds,
toasted and finely ground

12–16 live mussels

12–16 live clams

600 g/1 lb 5 oz thick boned hake
or cod fillets, skinned and cut
into 5-cm/2-inch chunks

12–16 raw prawns, peeled and
deveined

salt and pepper

thick crusty bread, to serve

Put the saffron threads in a heatproof jug with the water and
leave for at least 10 minutes to infuse.

Heat the oil in a large, heavy-based flameproof casserole over
a medium–high heat. Reduce the heat to low and cook the onion,
stirring occasionally, for 10 minutes, or until golden but not
browned. Stir in the garlic, thyme, bay leaves and red peppers
and cook, stirring frequently, for 5 minutes, or until the peppers
are softened and the onions have softened further.

Add the tomatoes and paprika and simmer, stirring frequently,
for a further 5 minutes.

Stir in the stock, the saffron and its soaking liquid and the
almonds and bring to the boil, stirring. Reduce the heat and
simmer for 5–10 minutes, until the sauce reduces and thickens.
Season to taste with salt and pepper.

Meanwhile, clean the mussels and clams by scrubbing or
scraping the shells and pulling out any beards that are attached
to the mussels. Discard any with broken shells or any that refuse
to close when tapped.

Gently stir the hake into the stew so that it doesn't break up,
then add the prawns, mussels and clams. Reduce the heat to very
low, cover and simmer for 5 minutes, or until the hake is opaque,
the mussels and clams have opened and the prawns have turned
pink. Discard any mussels or clams that remain closed. Serve
immediately with plenty of thick crusty bread for soaking up
the juices.

MEDITERRANEAN FISH STEW

Heat the oil in a large, flameproof casserole. Add the onion, saffron, thyme and a pinch of salt. Cook over a low heat, stirring occasionally, for 5 minutes, or until the onion has softened.

Add the garlic and cook for a further 2 minutes, then add the drained tomatoes and pour in the stock and wine. Season to taste with salt and pepper, bring the mixture to the boil, then reduce the heat and simmer for 15 minutes.

Add the chunks of mullet and monkfish and simmer for 3 minutes. Add the clams and squid and simmer for 5 minutes, or until the clam shells have opened. Discard any clams that remain closed. Tear the basil and stir it in. Serve garnished with the extra basil leaves.

SERVES 4

2 tbsp olive oil

1 onion, sliced

pinch of saffron threads, lightly crushed

1 tbsp chopped fresh thyme

2 garlic cloves, finely chopped

800 g/1 lb 12 oz canned chopped tomatoes, drained

2 litres/3½ pints fish stock

175 ml/6 fl oz dry white wine

350 g/12 oz red mullet fillets, cut into chunks

450 g/1 lb monkfish fillets, cut into chunks

450 g/1 lb fresh clams, scrubbed

225 g/8 oz squid rings

2 tbsp fresh basil leaves, plus extra to garnish

salt and pepper

PRAWN LAKSA

Peel and devein the prawns. Put the fish stock, salt and the prawn heads, peels and tails in a saucepan over a high heat and slowly bring to the boil. Lower the heat and simmer for 10 minutes.

Meanwhile, make the laksa paste. Put all the ingredients except the oil in a food processor and blend. With the motor running, slowly add up to 2 tablespoons of oil just until a paste forms. (If your food processor is too large to work efficiently with this small quantity, use a pestle and mortar, or make double the quantity and keep the leftovers tightly covered in the refrigerator to use another time.)

Heat the oil in a large saucepan over a high heat. Add the paste and stir-fry until it is fragrant. Strain the stock through a sieve lined with muslin. Stir the stock into the laksa paste, along with the coconut milk, nam pla and lime juice. Bring to the boil, then lower the heat, cover and simmer for 30 minutes.

Meanwhile, soak the noodles in a large bowl with enough lukewarm water to cover for 20 minutes, until soft. Alternatively, cook according to the packet instructions. Drain and set aside.

Add the prawns and beansprouts to the stew and continue simmering just until the prawns turn opaque and curl. Divide the noodles between 4 bowls and ladle the stew over, making sure everyone gets an equal share of the prawns. Garnish with the coriander and serve.

SERVES 4

20–24 large raw unpeeled prawns

450 ml/16 fl oz fish stock

pinch of salt

1 tsp groundnut oil

450 ml/16 fl oz coconut milk

2 tsp nam pla (Thai fish sauce)

½ tbsp lime juice

115 g/4 oz dried medium rice noodles

55 g/2 oz beansprouts

sprigs of fresh coriander, to garnish

laksa paste

6 coriander stalks with leaves

3 large garlic cloves, crushed

1 fresh red chilli, deseeded and chopped

1 lemon grass stalk, centre part only, chopped

2.5-cm/1-inch piece fresh ginger, peeled and chopped

1½ tbsp shrimp paste

½ tsp turmeric

2 tbsp groundnut oil

PRAWNS WITH COCONUT RICE

SERVES 4

- 15 g/¼ oz dried Chinese mushrooms
- 2 tbsp vegetable or groundnut oil
- 5 spring onions, chopped
- 55 g/2 oz desiccated coconut
- 1 fresh green chilli, deseeded and chopped
- 225 g/8 oz jasmine rice
- 150 ml/¼ pint fish stock
- 400 ml/14 fl oz coconut milk
- 350 g/12 oz cooked peeled prawns
- 5 sprigs fresh Thai basil

Place the mushrooms in a small bowl, cover with hot water and set aside to soak for 30 minutes. Drain, then cut off and discard the stalks and slice the caps.

Heat 1 tablespoon of the oil in a wok and stir-fry the spring onions, coconut and chilli for 2–3 minutes, until lightly browned. Add the mushrooms and stir-fry for 3–4 minutes.

Add the rice and stir-fry for 2–3 minutes, then add the stock and bring to the boil. Lower the heat and add the coconut milk. Simmer for 10–15 minutes, until the rice is tender. Stir in the prawns and basil, heat through and serve.

FISH & SEAFOOD

199

PRAWN BIRYANI

Soak the saffron in 50 ml/2 fl oz of tepid water for 10 minutes. Put the shallots, garlic, spices and salt into a spice grinder or mortar and pestle and grind to a paste.

Heat the ghee in a saucepan and add the mustard seeds. When they start to pop, add the prawns and stir over a high heat for 1 minute. Stir in the spice mix, then the coconut milk and yogurt. Simmer for 20 minutes.

Spoon the prawn mixture into serving bowls. Top with the freshly cooked basmati rice and drizzle over the saffron water. Serve, garnished with the flaked almonds, spring onion and sprigs of coriander.

SERVES 8

1 tsp saffron strands

2 shallots, roughly chopped

3 garlic cloves, crushed

1 tsp chopped fresh ginger

2 tsp coriander seeds

½ tsp black peppercorns

2 cloves

seeds from 2 green cardamom pods

1 tsp ground turmeric

1 fresh green chilli, chopped

½ tsp salt

2 tbsp ghee

1 tsp whole black mustard seeds

500 g/1 lb 2 oz raw tiger prawns

300 ml/½ pint coconut milk

300 ml/½ pint low-fat natural yogurt

freshly cooked basmati rice, to serve

to garnish

flaked almonds, toasted

1 spring onion, sliced

sprigs of fresh coriander

PRAWN & CHICKEN PAELLA

Soak the mussels in lightly salted water for 10 minutes. Put the saffron threads and water in a small bowl or cup and leave to infuse for a few minutes. Meanwhile, put the rice in a sieve and rinse in cold water until the water runs clear. Set aside.

Heat 3 tablespoons of the oil in a 30-cm/12-inch paella pan or ovenproof casserole. Cook the chicken thighs over a medium–high heat, turning frequently, for 5 minutes, or until golden and crispy. Using a slotted spoon, transfer to a bowl. Add the chorizo to the pan and cook, stirring, for 1 minute, or until beginning to crisp. Add to the chicken.

Heat the remaining oil in the pan and cook the onions, stirring frequently, for 2 minutes, then add the garlic and paprika and cook for a further 3 minutes, or until the onions are soft but not browned.

Add the drained rice, beans and peas and stir until coated in oil. Return the chicken and chorizo and any accumulated juices to the pan. Stir in the stock, saffron and its soaking liquid, and salt and pepper to taste and bring to the boil, stirring constantly. Reduce the heat to low and let simmer, uncovered and without stirring, for 15 minutes, or until the rice is almost tender.

Arrange the mussels, prawns and red peppers on top, then cover and simmer, without stirring, for a further 5 minutes, or until the prawns turn pink and the mussels open. Discard any mussels that remain closed. Taste and adjust the seasoning if necessary. Sprinkle with the parsley and serve immediately.

SERVES 6–8

- 16 live mussels
- ½ tsp saffron threads
- 2 tbsp hot water
- 350 g/12 oz cups paella rice
- 6 tbsp olive oil
- 6–8 boned chicken thighs
- 140 g/5 oz Spanish chorizo sausage, sliced
- 2 large onions, chopped
- 4 large garlic cloves, crushed
- 1 tsp mild or hot Spanish paprika
- 100 g/3½ oz green beans, chopped
- 125 g/4½ oz frozen peas
- 1.3 litres/2¼ pints fish stock
- 16 raw prawns, peeled and deveined
- 2 red peppers, halved and deseeded, then grilled, peeled and sliced
- salt and pepper
- 35 g/1¼ oz fresh chopped parsley, to garnish

MOULES MARINIÈRES

SERVES 4

2 kg/4 lb 8 oz live mussels
300 ml/10 fl oz dry white wine
6 shallots, finely chopped
1 bouquet garni
pepper
4 bay leaves, to garnish
crusty bread, to serve

Clean the mussels by scrubbing or scraping the shells and pulling off any beards. Discard any with broken shells or any that refuse to close when tapped with a knife. Rinse the mussels under cold running water.

Pour the wine into a large, heavy-based saucepan, add the shallots and bouquet garni and season to taste with pepper. Bring to the boil over a medium heat. Add the mussels, cover tightly and cook, shaking the saucepan occasionally, for 5 minutes. Remove and discard the bouquet garni and any mussels that remain closed. Divide the mussels between 4 serving bowls with a slotted spoon. Tilt the pan to let any sand settle, then spoon the cooking liquid over the mussels, garnish with a bay leaf, and serve immediately with bread.

SQUID WITH PARSLEY & PINE KERNELS

Place the sultanas in a small bowl, cover with lukewarm water and set aside for 15 minutes to plump up.

Meanwhile, heat the olive oil in a heavy-based saucepan. Add the parsley and garlic and cook over a low heat, stirring frequently, for 3 minutes. Add the squid and cook, stirring occasionally, for 5 minutes.

Increase the heat to medium, pour in the wine and cook until it has almost completely evaporated. Stir in the passata and season to taste with chilli powder and salt. Lower the heat, cover and simmer gently, stirring occasionally, for 45–50 minutes, until the squid is almost tender.

Drain the sultanas and stir them into the saucepan with the pine kernels. Leave to simmer for a further 10 minutes, then serve immediately, garnished with the reserved chopped parsley.

SERVES 4

- 85 g/3 oz sultanas
- 5 tbsp olive oil
- 6 tbsp chopped fresh flat-leaf parsley, plus extra to garnish
- 2 garlic cloves, finely chopped
- 800 g/1 lb 12 oz prepared squid, sliced, or squid rings
- 125 ml/4 fl oz dry white wine
- 500 g/1 lb 2 oz passata
- pinch of chilli powder
- 85 g/3 oz pine kernels, finely chopped
- salt

SEARED SCALLOPS IN GARLIC BROTH

Combine the garlic cloves, celery, carrot, onion, peppercorns, parsley stems and water in a saucepan with a good pinch of salt. Bring to the boil, reduce the heat and simmer, partially covered, for 30–45 minutes.

Strain the stock into a clean saucepan. Taste and adjust the seasoning, and keep hot.

If using sea scallops, slice in half horizontally to form 2 thinner rounds from each. (If the scallops are very large, slice them into 3 rounds.) Sprinkle with salt and pepper.

Heat the oil in a frying pan over a medium–high heat and cook the scallops on one side for 1–2 minutes, until lightly browned and the flesh becomes opaque.

Divide the scallops between 4 warmed shallow bowls, arranging them browned-side up. Ladle the stock over the scallops, then float a few coriander leaves on top. Serve immediately.

SERVES 4

1 large garlic bulb (about 100 g/ 3½ oz), separated into unpeeled cloves

1 celery stick, chopped

1 carrot, chopped

1 onion, chopped

10 peppercorns

5–6 parsley stems

1.2 litres/2 pints water

225 g/8 oz large sea scallops or queen scallops

1 tbsp oil

salt and pepper

fresh coriander leaves, to garnish

ROASTED SEAFOOD

oo g/1 lb 5 oz new potatoes

red onions, cut into wedges

courgettes, cut into chunks

garlic cloves, peeled but
left whole

lemons, cut into wedges

fresh rosemary sprigs

tbsp olive oil

50 g/12 oz unpeeled raw prawns

small raw squid, cut into rings

tomatoes, quartered

Preheat the oven to 200°C/400°F/Gas Mark 6.

Scrub the potatoes to remove any dirt. Cut any large potatoes
in half. Parboil the potatoes in a saucepan of boiling water for
10–15 minutes. Place the potatoes in a large roasting tin together
with the onions, courgettes, garlic, lemons and rosemary sprigs.

Pour over the oil and toss to coat all the vegetables. Roast in
the oven for 30 minutes, turning occasionally, until the potatoes
are tender.

Once the potatoes are tender, add the prawns, squid and
tomatoes, tossing to coat them in the oil, and roast for 5 minutes.
All the vegetables should be cooked through and slightly charred
for full flavour. Transfer the roasted seafood and vegetables to
warmed serving plates and serve hot.

FISH & SEAFOOD

211

SEAFOOD IN SAFFRON SAUCE

Clean the mussels and clams by scrubbing or scraping the shells and pulling out any beards that are attached to the mussels. Discard any with broken shells or any that refuse to close when tapped.

Heat the oil in a large, flameproof casserole and cook the onion with the saffron, thyme and a pinch of salt over a low heat, stirring occasionally, for 5 minutes, or until soft. Add the garlic and cook, stirring, for 2 minutes.

Add the tomatoes, wine and stock, season to taste with salt and pepper and stir well. Bring to the boil, then reduce the heat and simmer for 15 minutes.

Add the fish chunks and simmer for a further 3 minutes. Add the mussels, clams and squid rings and simmer for a further 5 minutes, or until the mussels and clams have opened. Discard any that remain closed. Stir in the basil and serve immediately, accompanied by plenty of fresh bread to mop up the broth.

SERVES 4

225 g/8 oz live mussels

225 g/8 oz live clams

2 tbsp olive oil

1 onion, sliced

pinch of saffron threads

1 tbsp chopped fresh thyme

2 garlic cloves, finely chopped

800 g/1 lb 12 oz canned tomatoes drained and chopped

175 ml/6 fl oz dry white wine

2 litres/3½ pints fish stock

350 g/12 oz red mullet fillets, cut into bite-sized chunks

450 g/1 lb monkfish fillets, cut into bite-sized chunks

225 g/8 oz raw squid rings

2 tbsp fresh shredded basil leaves

salt and pepper

fresh bread, to serve

SEAFOOD CHILLI

Place the prawns, scallops, monkfish chunks and lime slices in a large, non-metallic dish with ¼ teaspoon of the chilli powder, ¼ teaspoon of the ground cumin, 1 tablespoon of the chopped coriander, half the garlic, the fresh chilli and 1 tablespoon of the oil. Cover with clingfilm and leave to marinate for up to 1 hour.

Meanwhile, heat 1 tablespoon of the remaining oil in a flameproof casserole or large, heavy-based saucepan. Add the onion, the remaining garlic and the red and yellow peppers and cook over a low heat, stirring occasionally, for 5 minutes, or until softened.

Add the remaining chilli powder, the remaining cumin, the cloves, cinnamon and cayenne pepper, and the remaining oil, if needed, and season to taste with salt. Cook, stirring, for 5 minutes, then gradually stir in the stock and the tomatoes and their juices. Partially cover and simmer for 25 minutes.

Add the beans to the tomato mixture and spoon the fish and shellfish on top. Cover and cook for 10 minutes, or until the fish and shellfish are cooked through. Sprinkle with the remaining coriander and serve.

SERVES 4

- 115 g/4 oz raw prawns, peeled
- 250 g/9 oz prepared scallops, thawed if frozen
- 115 g/4 oz monkfish fillet, cut into chunks
- 1 lime, peeled and thinly sliced
- 1 tbsp chilli powder
- 1 tsp ground cumin
- 3 tbsp chopped fresh coriander
- 2 garlic cloves, finely chopped
- 1 fresh green chilli, deseeded and chopped
- 3 tbsp corn oil
- 1 onion, roughly chopped
- 1 red and 1 yellow pepper, deseeded and chopped
- ½ tsp ground cloves
- pinch of ground cinnamon
- pinch of cayenne pepper
- 350 ml/12 fl oz fish stock
- 400 g/14 oz canned chopped tomatoes
- 400 g/14 oz canned red kidney beans, drained and rinsed
- salt

MOROCCAN FISH TAGINE

SERVES 4

2 tbsp olive oil

1 large onion, finely chopped

pinch of saffron threads

½ tsp ground cinnamon

1 tsp ground coriander

½ tsp ground cumin

½ tsp ground turmeric

200 g/7 oz canned chopped
   tomatoes

300 ml/10 fl oz fish stock

4 small red mullet, cleaned, boned
   and heads and tails removed

55 g/2 oz stoned green olives

1 tbsp chopped preserved lemon

3 tbsp chopped fresh coriander

salt and pepper

freshly cooked couscous,
   to serve

Heat the olive oil in a flameproof casserole. Add the onion and cook gently over a very low heat, stirring occasionally, for 10 minutes, or until softened, but not coloured. Add the saffron, cinnamon, ground coriander, cumin and turmeric and cook for a further 30 seconds, stirring constantly.

Add the tomatoes and fish stock and stir well. Bring to the boil, reduce the heat, cover and simmer for 15 minutes. Uncover and simmer for 20–35 minutes, or until thickened.

Cut each red mullet in half, then add the fish pieces to the casserole, pushing them down into the liquid. Simmer the stew for a further 5–6 minutes, or until the fish is just cooked.

Carefully stir in the olives, preserved lemon and chopped coriander. Season to taste with salt and pepper and serve immediately with couscous.

GOAN-STYLE SEAFOOD CURRY

Heat the oil in a wok or large frying pan over a high heat. Add the mustard seeds and stir them around for about 1 minute, or until they jump. Stir in the curry leaves.

Add the shallots and garlic and stir for about 5 minutes, or until the shallots are golden. Stir in the turmeric, coriander and chilli powder and continue stirring for about 30 seconds.

Add the dissolved creamed coconut. Bring to the boil, then reduce the heat to medium and stir for about 2 minutes.

Reduce the heat to low, add the fish and simmer for 1 minute, spooning the sauce over the fish and very gently stirring it around. Add the prawns and continue to simmer for 4–5 minutes longer until the fish flesh flakes easily and the prawns turn pink and curl.

Add half the lime juice, then taste and add more lime juice and salt to taste. Sprinkle with the lime rind and serve with lime wedges.

SERVES 4–6

3 tbsp vegetable or groundnut oil

1 tbsp black mustard seeds

12 fresh curry leaves or
   1 tbsp dried

6 shallots, finely chopped

1 garlic clove, crushed

1 tsp ground turmeric

½ tsp ground coriander

¼–½ tsp chilli powder

140 g/5 oz creamed coconut,
   grated and dissolved in
   300 ml/10 fl oz boiling water

500 g/1 lb 2 oz skinless, boneless
   white fish, such as monkfish or
   cod, cut into large chunks

450 g/1 lb large raw prawns,
   peeled and deveined

finely grated rind and juice
   of 1 lime

salt

lime wedges, to serve

VEGETABLES

RATATOUILLE

Heat the oil in a large saucepan. Add the onions and cook over a low heat, stirring occasionally, for 5 minutes, or until softened. Add the garlic and cook, stirring frequently for a further 2 minutes.

Add the aubergines, courgettes and peppers. Increase the heat to medium and cook, stirring occasionally, until the peppers begin to colour. Add the bouquet garni, reduce the heat, cover and simmer gently for 40 minutes.

Stir in the chopped tomatoes and season to taste with salt and pepper. Re-cover the saucepan and simmer gently for a further 10 minutes. Remove and discard the bouquet garni. Serve warm or cold.

SERVES 4

150 ml/5 fl oz olive oil

2 onions, sliced

2 garlic cloves, finely chopped

2 medium-sized aubergines, roughly chopped

4 courgettes, roughly chopped

2 yellow peppers, deseeded and chopped

2 red peppers, deseeded and chopped

1 bouquet garni,

3 large tomatoes, peeled, deseeded and roughly chopped

salt and pepper

ROAST SUMMER VEGETABLES

Preheat the oven to 200°C/400°F/Gas Mark 6. Brush a large ovenproof dish with a little of the oil. Arrange the prepared vegetables in the dish and tuck the garlic cloves and rosemary sprigs among them. Drizzle with the remaining oil and season to taste with plenty of pepper.

Roast the vegetables in the preheated oven for 20–25 minutes, turning once, until they are tender and beginning to turn golden brown.

Serve the vegetables immediately, straight from the dish or transferred to a warmed serving platter, accompanied by crusty bread, if you like, to mop up the juices.

SERVES 4

150 ml/5 fl oz olive oil

1 fennel bulb, cut into wedges

2 red onions, cut into wedges

2 beef tomatoes, cut into wedges

1 aubergine, thickly sliced

2 courgettes, thickly sliced

1 yellow pepper, deseeded and cut into chunks

1 red pepper, deseeded and cut into chunks

1 orange pepper, deseeded and cut into chunks

4 garlic cloves

4 fresh rosemary sprigs

pepper

crusty bread, to serve (optional)

POTATO & MUSHROOM PIE

SERVES 4

tbsp butter

00 g/1 lb 2 oz waxy potatoes,
thinly sliced and parboiled

50 g/5½ oz sliced mixed
mushrooms

tbsp chopped fresh rosemary,
plus extra to garnish

tbsp snipped chives, plus extra
to garnish

garlic cloves, crushed

50 ml/5 fl oz double cream

alt and pepper

Preheat the oven to 190°C/375°F/Gas Mark 5. Grease a shallow,
round ovenproof dish with the butter.

Layer a quarter of the potatoes in the base of the dish. Arrange
one third of the mushrooms on top of the potatoes and sprinkle
with one third of the rosemary, chives and garlic. Continue
making the layers in the same order, and finish with a layer of
potatoes on top.

Pour the double cream evenly over the top of the potatoes.
Season to taste with salt and pepper.

Place the dish in the preheated oven, and cook for about
45 minutes, or until the pie is golden brown and piping hot.

Garnish with snipped chives and serve immediately, straight
from the dish.

AUBERGINE GRATIN

Heat the oil in a flameproof casserole over a medium heat. Add the onion and cook for 5 minutes, or until soft. Add the garlic and cook for a few seconds, or until just beginning to colour. Using a perforated spoon, transfer the onion mixture to a plate.

Cook the aubergine slices in batches in the same flameproof casserole until they are just lightly browned. Transfer to another plate.

Preheat the oven to 200°C/400°F/Gas Mark 6. Arrange a layer of aubergine slices in the base of the casserole dish or a shallow ovenproof dish. Sprinkle with some of the parsley, thyme, salt and pepper. Add layers of onion, tomatoes and mozzarella, sprinkling parsley, thyme, salt and pepper over each layer.

Continue layering, finishing with a layer of aubergine slices. Sprinkle with the Parmesan. Bake, uncovered, in the preheated oven for 20–30 minutes, or until the top is golden and the aubergines are tender. Serve hot.

SERVES 2

4 tbsp olive oil

2 onions, finely chopped

2 garlic cloves, very finely chopped

2 aubergines, thickly sliced

3 tbsp chopped fresh flat-leaf parsley

½ tsp dried thyme

400 g/14 oz canned chopped tomatoes

175 g/6 oz mozzarella, coarsely grated

6 tbsp freshly grated Parmesan cheese

salt and pepper

PARMESAN RISOTTO WITH MUSHROOMS

Heat the oil in a deep saucepan. Add the rice and cook over a low heat, stirring constantly, for 2–3 minutes, until the grains are thoroughly coated in oil and translucent.

Add the garlic, onion, celery and pepper and cook, stirring frequently, for 5 minutes. Add the mushrooms and cook for 3–4 minutes. Stir in the oregano.

Gradually add the hot stock, a ladle at a time. Stir constantly and add more liquid as the rice absorbs each addition. Increase the heat to medium so that the liquid bubbles. Cook for 20 minutes, or until all the liquid is absorbed and the rice is creamy. Add the sun-dried tomatoes, if using, 5 minutes before the end of the cooking time and season to taste with salt and pepper.

Remove the risotto from the heat and stir in half the Parmesan until it melts. Transfer the risotto to warmed bowls. Top with the remaining cheese, garnish with flat-leaf parsley and serve immediately.

SERVES 6

2 tbsp olive oil or vegetable oil

225 g/8 oz risotto rice

2 garlic cloves, crushed

1 onion, chopped

2 celery sticks, chopped

1 red or green pepper, deseeded and chopped

225 g/8 oz mushrooms, thinly sliced

1 tbsp chopped fresh oregano or 1 tsp dried oregano

1 litre/1¾ pints vegetable stock

55 g /2 oz sun-dried tomatoes in olive oil, drained and chopped (optional)

55 g/2 oz finely grated Parmesan cheese

salt and pepper

fresh flat-leaf parsley sprigs or bay leaves, to garnish

RISOTTO WITH ARTICHOKE HEARTS

225 g/8 oz canned artichoke
    hearts
1 tbsp olive oil
40 g/1½ oz butter
1 small onion, finely chopped
280 g/10 oz risotto rice
1.2 litres/2 pints hot vegetable
    stock
85 g/3 oz freshly grated Parmesan
    cheese or Grana Padano cheese
salt and pepper
fresh flat-leaf parsley sprigs,
    to garnish

Drain the artichoke hearts, reserving the liquid, and cut them
into quarters.

Heat the oil with 25 g/1 oz of the butter in a deep saucepan
over a medium heat until the butter has melted. Stir in the onion
and cook gently, stirring occasionally, for 5 minutes, or until soft
and starting to turn golden. Do not brown.

Add the rice and mix to coat in oil and butter. Cook, stirring
constantly, for 2–3 minutes, or until the grains are translucent.

Gradually add the artichoke liquid and the hot stock, a ladle at
a time. Stir constantly and add more liquid as the rice absorbs
each addition. Increase the heat to medium so that the liquid
bubbles. Cook for 15 minutes, then add the artichoke hearts.
Cook for a further 5 minutes, or until all the liquid is absorbed
and the rice is creamy. Season to taste with salt and pepper.

Remove the risotto from the heat and add the remaining
butter. Mix well, then stir in the cheese until it melts. Season, if
necessary. Spoon the risotto into warmed bowls, garnish with
parsley sprigs and serve immediately.

VEGETARIAN PAELLA

Put the saffron threads and water in a small bowl or cup and leave to infuse for a few minutes.

Meanwhile, heat the oil in a paella pan or wide, shallow frying pan and cook the onion over a medium heat, stirring, for 2–3 minutes, or until softened. Add the garlic, peppers and aubergine and cook, stirring frequently, for 5 minutes.

Add the rice and cook, stirring constantly, for 1 minute, or until glossy and coated. Pour in the stock and add the tomatoes, saffron and its soaking water, and salt and pepper to taste. Bring to the boil, then reduce the heat and leave to simmer, shaking the frying pan frequently and stirring occasionally, for 15 minutes.

Stir in the mushrooms, French beans and pinto beans with their can juices. Cook for a further 10 minutes, then serve immediately.

SERVES 4–6

½ tsp saffron threads

2 tbsp hot water

6 tbsp olive oil

1 Spanish onion, sliced

3 garlic cloves, minced

1 red pepper, deseeded and sliced

1 orange pepper, deseeded and sliced

1 large aubergine, cubed

200 g/7 oz medium-grain paella rice

600 ml/1 pint vegetable stock

450 g/1 lb tomatoes, peeled and chopped

115 g/4 oz button mushrooms, sliced

115 g/4 oz French beans, halved

400 g/14 oz canned pinto beans

salt and pepper

EGG-FRIED RICE WITH VEGETABLES

Heat the oil in a wok or large frying pan and fry the garlic and chillies for 2–3 minutes.

Add the mushrooms, mangetout and baby sweetcorn and stir-fry for 2–3 minutes before adding the soy sauce, sugar and basil. Stir in the rice.

Push the mixture to one side of the wok. Add the eggs to the wok and stir until lightly set before combining with the rice mixture.

If you wish to make the optional crispy onion topping, heat the oil in another frying pan and sauté the onions until crispy and brown. Serve the rice topped with the onions.

SERVES 4

- 2 tbsp vegetable or groundnut oil
- 2 garlic cloves, finely chopped
- 2 fresh red chillies, deseeded and chopped
- 115 g/4 oz mushrooms, sliced
- 50 g/2 oz mangetout, halved
- 50 g/2 oz baby sweetcorn, halved
- 3 tbsp Thai soy sauce
- 1 tbsp palm sugar or soft, light brown sugar
- a few Thai basil leaves
- 350 g/12 oz rice, cooked and cooled
- 2 eggs, beaten

crispy onion topping (optional)

- 2 tbsp vegetable or groundnut oil
- 2 onions, sliced

SPICED BASMATI PILAU

SERVES 4

500 g/1 lb 2 oz basmati rice

175 g/6 oz broccoli, trimmed

5 tbsp vegetable oil

2 large onions, chopped

225 g/8 oz mushrooms, sliced

2 garlic cloves, crushed

6 cardamom pods, split

6 whole cloves

8 black peppercorns

1 cinnamon stick or piece of cassia bark

1 tsp turmeric

1.2 litres/2 pints vegetable stock or water

50 g/2 oz seedless raisins

50 g/2 oz unsalted pistachio nuts, roughly chopped

salt and pepper

Place the rice in a sieve and wash well under cold running water. Drain. Trim off most of the broccoli stalk and cut the head into small florets, then quarter the stalk lengthways and cut diagonally into 1-cm/½-inch pieces.

Heat the oil in a large saucepan. Add the onions and broccoli stalks and cook over a low heat, stirring frequently, for 3 minutes. Add the mushrooms, rice, garlic and spices and cook for 1 minute, stirring, until the rice is coated in oil.

Add the stock and season to taste with salt and pepper. Stir in the broccoli florets and return the mixture to the boil. Cover, reduce the heat and cook over a low heat for 15 minutes without uncovering the pan.

Remove the pan from the heat and leave the pilau to stand for 5 minutes without uncovering. Remove the whole spices, add the raisins and pistachios and gently fork through to fluff up the grains. Serve the pilau hot.

MOROCCAN STEW

Heat the oil in a large, heavy-based saucepan with a tight-fitting lid and cook the onion, garlic, chilli and aubergine, stirring frequently, for 5–8 minutes until softened.

Add the cumin, coriander and saffron and cook, stirring constantly, for 2 minutes. Bruise the cinnamon stick.

Add the cinnamon, squash, sweet potatoes, prunes, 450 ml/ 16 fl oz stock and the tomatoes to the saucepan and bring to the boil. Reduce the heat, cover and simmer, stirring occasionally, for 20 minutes. Add the chickpeas to the saucepan and cook for a further 10 minutes, adding more stock if necessary. Discard the cinnamon and serve garnished with the fresh coriander.

SERVES 4

- 2 tbsp olive oil
- 1 Spanish onion, finely chopped
- 2–4 garlic cloves, crushed
- 1 fresh red chilli, deseeded and sliced
- 1 aubergine, about 225 g/8 oz, cut into small chunks
- 1 tsp ground cumin
- 1 tsp ground coriander
- pinch of saffron threads
- 1–2 cinnamon sticks
- ½–1 butternut squash, about 450 g/1 lb, peeled, deseeded and cut into small chunks
- 225 g/8 oz sweet potatoes, cut into small chunks
- 85 g/3 oz ready-to-eat prunes
- 450–600 ml/16 fl oz–1 pint vegetable stock
- 4 tomatoes, chopped
- 400 g/14 oz canned chickpeas, drained and rinsed
- 1 tbsp chopped fresh coriander, to garnish

POTATO & LEMON CASSEROLE

Heat the olive oil in a flameproof casserole. Add the onions and sauté over a medium heat, stirring frequently, for 3 minutes.

Add the garlic and cook for 30 seconds. Stir in the ground cumin, ground coriander and cayenne and cook, stirring constantly, for 1 minute.

Add the carrot, turnips, courgette and potatoes and stir to coat in the oil.

Add the lemon juice and rind and the stock. Season to taste with salt and pepper. Cover and cook over a medium heat, stirring occasionally, for 20–30 minutes until tender.

Remove the lid, sprinkle in the chopped fresh coriander and stir well. Serve immediately.

SERVES 4

100 ml/3½ fl oz olive oil

2 red onions, cut into 8 wedges

3 garlic cloves, crushed

2 tsp ground cumin

2 tsp ground coriander

pinch of cayenne pepper

1 carrot, thickly sliced

2 small turnips, quartered

1 courgette, sliced

500 g/1 lb 2 oz potatoes, thickly sliced

juice and grated rind of 2 large lemons

300 ml/10 fl oz vegetable stock

2 tbsp chopped fresh coriander

salt and pepper

LENTIL & RICE CASSEROLE

SERVES 4

25 g/8 oz red lentils

5 g/2 oz long-grain rice

2 litres/2 pints vegetable stock

leek, cut into chunks

garlic cloves, crushed

oo g/14 oz canned chopped
tomatoes

tsp ground cumin

tsp chilli powder

tsp garam masala

red pepper, deseeded and sliced

oo g/3½ oz small broccoli florets

baby sweetcorn, halved
lengthways

5 g/2 oz French beans, halved

tbsp shredded fresh basil

alt and pepper

resh basil sprigs, to garnish

Place the lentils, rice and stock in a large flameproof casserole
and cook over a low heat, stirring occasionally, for 20 minutes.

Add the leek, garlic, tomatoes and their can juice, ground
cumin, chilli powder, garam masala, sliced pepper, broccoli, baby
sweetcorn and French beans to the pan.

Bring the mixture to the boil, reduce the heat, cover and
simmer for a further 10–15 minutes or until the vegetables
are tender.

Add the shredded basil and season to taste with salt
and pepper.

Garnish with fresh basil sprigs and serve immediately.

VEGETABLE GOULASH

Put the sun-dried tomatoes in a small heatproof bowl, cover with almost boiling water and leave to soak for 15–20 minutes. Drain, reserving the soaking liquid.

Heat the oil in a large, heavy-based saucepan, with a tight-fitting lid, and cook the chillies, garlic and vegetables, stirring frequently, for 5–8 minutes until softened. Blend the tomato purée with a little of the stock in a jug and pour over the vegetable mixture, then add the remaining stock, lentils, the sun-dried tomatoes and their soaking liquid, and the paprika and thyme.

Bring to the boil, then reduce the heat, cover and simmer for 15 minutes. Add the fresh tomatoes and simmer for a further 15 minutes, or until the vegetables and lentils are tender. Serve topped with spoonfuls of soured cream, accompanied by crusty bread.

SERVES 4

15 g/½ oz sun-dried tomatoes, chopped

2 tbsp olive oil

½–1 tsp crushed dried chillies

2–3 garlic cloves, chopped

1 large onion, cut into small wedges

1 small celeriac, cut into small chunks

225 g/8 oz carrots, sliced

225 g/8 oz new potatoes, scrubbed and cut into chunks

1 small acorn squash, deseeded, peeled and cut into small chunks, about 225 g/8 oz prepared weight

2 tbsp tomato purée

300 ml/10 fl oz vegetable stock

450 g/1 lb canned Puy or green lentils, drained and rinsed

1–2 tsp hot paprika

a few sprigs fresh thyme

450 g/1 lb ripe tomatoes

soured cream, to garnish

crusty bread, to serve

RIBOLLITA

Heat the oil in a large saucepan and cook the onions, carrots and celery for 10–15 minutes, stirring frequently. Add the garlic, thyme, and salt and pepper to taste. Continue to cook for a further

1–2 minutes, until the vegetables are golden and caramelized.

Add the cannellini beans to the pan and pour in the tomatoes. Add enough of the water to cover the vegetables.

Bring to the boil and simmer for 20 minutes. Add the parsley and cavolo nero and cook for a further 5 minutes.

Stir in the bread and add a little more water, if needed. The consistency should be thick.

Taste and adjust the seasoning, if needed. Ladle into warmed serving bowls and serve hot, drizzled with extra virgin olive oil.

SERVES 4

3 tbsp olive oil

2 medium red onions, roughly chopped

3 carrots, sliced

3 celery sticks, roughly chopped

3 garlic cloves, chopped

1 tbsp chopped fresh thyme

400 g/14 oz canned cannellini beans, drained and rinsed

400 g/14 oz canned chopped tomatoes

600 ml/1 pint water or vegetable stock

2 tbsp chopped fresh parsley

500 g/1 lb 2 oz cavolo nero or Savoy cabbage, trimmed and sliced

1 small day-old ciabatta loaf, torn into small pieces

salt and pepper

extra virgin olive oil, to serve

VEGETABLE STEW WITH PESTO

SERVES 6

- tbsp olive oil
- onion, finely chopped
- large leek, thinly sliced
- celery stick, thinly sliced
- carrot, quartered and thinly sliced
- garlic clove, finely chopped
- .4 litres/2½ pints water
- potato, diced
- parsnip, finely diced
- small kohlrabi or turnip, diced
- 50 g/5½ oz French beans, cut in small pieces
- 50 g/5½ oz fresh or frozen peas
- 2 small courgettes, quartered lengthways and sliced
- 400 g/14 oz canned flageolet beans, drained and rinsed
- .00 g/3½ oz spinach leaves, cut into thin ribbons
- eady-made pesto
- salt and pepper

Heat the olive oil in a large saucepan over a medium–low heat. Add the onion and leek and cook for 5 minutes, stirring occasionally, until the onion softens. Add the celery, carrot and garlic and cook, covered, for a further 5 minutes, stirring frequently.

Add the water, potato, parsnip, kohlrabi and French beans. Bring to the boil, reduce the heat to low and simmer, covered, for 5 minutes.

Add the peas, courgettes and flageolet beans, and season generously with salt and pepper. Cover again and simmer for about 25 minutes until all the vegetables are tender.

Add the spinach and simmer for a further 5 minutes. Taste and adjust the seasoning and stir in about a tablespoon of the pesto. Ladle into warmed bowls and serve with the remaining pesto.

VEGETABLE STEW WITH GREEN LENTILS

Heat the oil in a large saucepan over a medium heat, add the onion, garlic and carrot and cook for 3–4 minutes, stirring frequently, until the onion starts to soften. Add the cabbage and cook for a further 2 minutes.

Add the tomatoes, thyme and 1 bay leaf, then pour in the stock. Bring to the boil, reduce the heat to low and cook gently, partially covered, for about 45 minutes until the vegetables are tender.

Meanwhile, put the lentils in another saucepan with the remaining bay leaf and the water. Bring just to the boil, reduce the heat and simmer for about 25 minutes until tender. Drain off any remaining water, and set aside.

Allow the stew to cool, then transfer to a food processor or blender and process until smooth, working in batches, if necessary. (If using a food processor, strain off the cooking liquid and reserve. Purée the solids with enough cooking liquid to moisten them, then combine with the remaining liquid.)

Return the stew to the saucepan and add the cooked lentils. Taste and adjust the seasoning, and cook for about 10 minutes to heat through. Ladle into warmed bowls and garnish with parsley.

SERVES 6

1 tbsp olive oil

1 onion, finely chopped

1 garlic clove, finely chopped

1 carrot, halved and thinly sliced

450 g/1 lb young green cabbage, cored, quartered and thinly sliced

400 g/14 oz canned chopped tomatoes

½ tsp dried thyme

2 bay leaves

1.5 litres/2¾ pints chicken or vegetable stock

200 g/7 oz Puy lentils

450 ml/16 fl oz water

salt and pepper

chopped fresh parsley, to garnish

SPRING STEW

Heat the oil in a large, heavy-based saucepan with a tight-fitting lid. Add the onions, celery, carrots and potatoes and cook, stirring frequently, for 5 minutes, or until softened. Add the stock, drained beans, bouquet garni and soy sauce, then bring to the boil. Reduce the heat, cover and simmer for 12 minutes.

Add the baby sweetcorn and broad beans and season to taste with salt and pepper. Simmer for a further 3 minutes.

Meanwhile, discard the outer leaves and hard central core from the cabbage and shred the leaves. Add to the saucepan and simmer for a further 3–5 minutes, or until all the vegetables are tender.

Blend the cornflour with the water, stir into the saucepan and cook, stirring, for 4–6 minutes, or until the liquid has thickened. Serve with a bowl of Parmesan cheese for stirring into the stew.

SERVES 4

2 tbsp olive oil

4–8 baby onions, halved

1 celery sticks, sliced

225 g/8 oz baby carrots, scrubbed, and halved if large

300 g/10½ oz new potatoes, scrubbed and halved, or quartered if large

850 ml–1.2 litres/1½–2 pints vegetable stock

400 g/14 oz canned haricot beans drained and rinsed

1 fresh bouquet garni

1½–2 tbsp light soy sauce

85 g/3 oz baby sweetcorn

115 g/4 oz frozen or shelled fresh broad beans, thawed if frozen

½–1 Savoy or spring cabbage, about 225 g/8 oz

1½ tbsp cornflour

2 tbsp cold water

salt and pepper

55–85 g/2–3 oz Parmesan, grated, to serve

CHILLI BEAN STEW

SERVES 4–6

2 tbsp olive oil

1 onion, chopped

4 garlic cloves, chopped

2 fresh red chillies, deseeded and sliced

425 g/8 oz canned kidney beans, drained and rinsed

425 g/8 oz canned cannellini beans, drained and rinsed

425 g/8 oz canned chickpeas, drained and rinsed

2 tbsp tomato purée

600–850 ml/1¼–1½ pints vegetable stock

1 red pepper, deseeded and chopped

2 tomatoes, roughly chopped

175 g/6 oz frozen or shelled fresh broad beans, thawed if frozen

2 tbsp chopped fresh coriander, plus extra to garnish

pepper

soured cream, to serve

paprika, to garnish

Heat the oil in a large, heavy-based saucepan with a tight-fitting lid and cook the onion, garlic and chillies, stirring frequently, for 5 minutes, or until softened. Add the kidney beans and cannellini beans and the chickpeas. Blend the tomato purée with a little of the stock in a jug and pour over the bean mixture, then add the remaining stock. Bring to the boil, then reduce the heat and simmer for 10–15 minutes.

Add the red pepper, tomatoes, broad beans, and pepper to taste and simmer for a further 15–20 minutes, or until all the vegetables are tender. Stir in the chopped coriander.

Serve the stew topped with spoonfuls of soured cream and garnished with chopped coriander and a pinch of paprika.

VEGETABLES

257

TUSCAN BEAN STEW

Trim the fennel and reserve any feathery fronds, then cut the bulb into small strips. Heat the oil in a large, heavy-based saucepan with a tight-fitting lid, and cook the onion, garlic, chilli and the fennel strips, stirring frequently, for 5–8 minutes, or until softened.

Add the aubergine and cook, stirring frequently, for 5 minutes. Blend the tomato purée with a little of the stock in a jug and pour over the fennel mixture, then add the remaining stock, and the tomatoes, vinegar and oregano. Bring to the boil, then reduce the heat, cover and simmer for 15 minutes, or until the tomatoes have begun to collapse.

Drain and rinse the beans, the drain again. Add them to the pan with the yellow pepper, courgette and olives. Simmer for a further 15 minutes, or until all the vegetables are tender. Taste and adjust the seasoning. Scatter with the Parmesan cheese shavings and serve garnished with the reserved fennel fronds, accompanied by crusty bread.

SERVES 4

1 large fennel bulb

2 tbsp olive oil

1 red onion, cut into small wedge

2–4 garlic cloves, sliced

1 fresh green chilli, deseeded an
    chopped

1 small aubergine, about 225 g/
    8 oz, cut into chunks

2 tbsp tomato purée

600 ml/1 pint vegetable stock

450 g/1 lb ripe tomatoes

1 tbsp balsamic vinegar

a few sprigs fresh oregano

400 g/14 oz canned borlotti bean

400 g/14 oz canned flageolet
    beans

1 yellow pepper, deseeded and c
    into small strips

1 courgette, sliced into half moo

55 g/2 oz stoned black olives

25 g/1 oz Parmesan cheese,
    freshly shaved

salt and pepper

crusty bread, to serve

KIDNEY BEAN, PUMPKIN & TOMATO STEW

Pick over the beans, cover generously with cold water and leave to soak for 6 hours or overnight. Drain the beans, put in a saucepan and add enough cold water to cover by 5 cm/2 inches. Bring to the boil and boil for 10 minutes. Drain and rinse well.

Heat the oil in a large saucepan over a medium heat. Add the onions, cover and cook for 3–4 minutes, until they are just softened, stirring occasionally. Add the garlic, celery and carrot, and continue cooking for 2 minutes.

Add the water, drained beans, tomato purée, thyme, oregano, cumin and bay leaf. When the mixture begins to bubble, reduce the heat to low. Cover and simmer gently for 1 hour, stirring occasionally.

Stir in the tomatoes, pumpkin and chilli purée and continue simmering for a further hour, or until the beans and pumpkin are tender, stirring from time to time.

Season to taste with salt and pepper and stir in a little more chilli purée, if liked. Ladle the soup into bowls, garnish with coriander and serve.

SERVES 4–6

250 g/9 oz dried kidney beans

1 tbsp olive oil

2 onions, finely chopped

4 garlic cloves, finely chopped

1 celery stick, thinly sliced

1 carrot, halved and thinly sliced

1.2 litres/2 pints water

2 tsp tomato purée

⅛ tsp dried thyme

⅛ tsp dried oregano

⅛ tsp ground cumin

1 bay leaf

400 g/14 oz canned chopped tomatoes

250 g/9 oz peeled pumpkin flesh, diced

¼ tsp chilli purée, or to taste

salt and pepper

fresh coriander leaves, to garnish

BEANS &
GREENS STEW

SERVES 4

250 g/9 oz dried haricot or
   cannellini beans

4 tbsp olive oil

2 onions, finely chopped

4 garlic cloves, finely chopped

1 celery stick, thinly sliced

2 carrots, halved and thinly sliced

1.2 litres/2 pints water

¼ tsp dried thyme

¼ tsp dried marjoram

1 bay leaf

125 g/4½ oz leafy greens, such
   as chard, mustard, spinach and
   kale, washed

salt and pepper

Pick over the beans, cover generously with cold water and
leave to soak for 6 hours or overnight. Drain the beans, put in a
saucepan and add enough cold water to cover by 5 cm/2 inches.
Bring to the boil and boil for 10 minutes. Drain and rinse well.

Heat the oil in a large saucepan over a medium heat. Add the
onions and cook, covered, for 3–4 minutes, stirring occasionally,
until the onions are just softened. Add the garlic, celery and
carrots, and continue cooking for 2 minutes.

Add the water, drained beans, thyme, marjoram and bay leaf.
When the mixture begins to bubble, reduce the heat to low. Cover
and simmer gently, stirring occasionally, for about 1¼ hours until
the beans are tender; the cooking time will vary depending on
the type of bean. Season with salt and pepper.

Allow the soup to cool slightly, then transfer 450 ml/16 fl oz to
a food processor or blender. Process until smooth and recombine
with the stew.

A handful at a time, cut the greens crossways into thin ribbons,
keeping tender leaves like spinach separate. Add the thicker
leaves and cook gently, uncovered, for 10 minutes. Stir in any
remaining greens and continue cooking for 5–10 minutes, until all
the greens are tender.

Taste and adjust the seasoning, if necessary. Ladle the stew
into warmed bowls and serve.

HOT & SOUR NOODLES WITH TOFU

Put the lime rind, garlic and ginger into a large saucepan with the stock and bring to the boil. Reduce the heat and simmer for 5 minutes. Remove the lime rind, garlic and ginger with a slotted spoon and discard.

Meanwhile, heat the vegetable oil in a large frying pan over a high heat, add the tofu and cook, turning frequently, until golden. Remove from the pan and drain on kitchen paper.

Add the noodles, mushrooms and chilli to the stock and simmer for 3 minutes. Add the tofu, spring onions, soy sauce, lime juice, rice wine and sesame oil and briefly heat through.

Divide between 4 warmed bowls, scatter over the coriander and serve immediately.

SERVES 4

- 3 strips lime rind
- 2 garlic cloves, peeled
- 2 slices fresh ginger
- 1 litre/1¾ pints chicken stock
- 1 tbsp vegetable oil
- 150 g/5½ oz firm tofu (drained weight), cubed
- 200 g/7 oz dried fine egg noodles
- 100 g/3½ oz shiitake mushrooms, sliced
- 1 fresh red chilli, deseeded and sliced
- 4 spring onions, sliced
- 1 tsp soy sauce
- juice of 1 lime
- 1 tsp Chinese rice wine
- 1 tsp sesame oil
- chopped fresh coriander, to garnish

DESSERTS

APPLE &
BLACKBERRY
CRUMBLE

Preheat the oven to 190°C/375°F/Gas Mark 5.

Peel and core the apples and cut into chunks. Place in a bowl with the blackberries, muscovado sugar and cinnamon and mix together, then transfer to an ovenproof baking dish.

To make the crumble topping, sift the self-raising flour into a bowl and stir in the wholemeal flour. Add the unsalted butter and rub in with your fingers until the mixture resembles fine breadcrumbs. Stir in the demerara sugar.

Spread the crumble over the apples and bake in the preheated oven for 40–45 minutes, or until the apples are soft and the crumble is golden brown and crisp.

Serve hot with cream.

SERVES 4

900 g/2 lb cooking apples, peeled and sliced

300 g/10½ oz blackberries, fresh or frozen

55 g/2 oz light muscovado sugar

1 tsp ground cinnamon

single or double cream, to serve

crumble topping

85 g/3 oz self-raising flour

85 g/3 oz plain wholemeal flour

115 g/4 oz unsalted butter

55 g/2 oz demerara sugar

RHUBARB
CRUMBLE

Preheat the oven to 190°C/375°F/Gas Mark 5.

Cut the rhubarb into 2.5-cm/1-inch lengths and place in a
1.7-litre/3-pint ovenproof dish with the sugar and the orange
rind and juice.

Make the crumble topping by placing the flour in a mixing bowl
and rubbing in the unsalted butter until the mixture resembles
breadcrumbs. Stir in the sugar and the ginger.

Spread the crumble evenly over the fruit and press down lightly
using a fork. Bake in the centre of the oven on a baking tray for
25–30 minutes until the crumble is golden brown.

Serve warm with cream.

SERVES 6

900 g/2 lb rhubarb

115 g/4 oz caster sugar

grated rind and juice of
  1 orange

cream, yogurt or custard,
  to serve

crumble topping

225 g/8 oz plain or
  wholemeal flour

115 g/4 oz unsalted butter

115 g/4 oz soft brown sugar

1 tsp ground ginger

APRICOT CRUMBLE

SERVES 6

5 g/2½ oz unsalted butter,
plus extra for greasing

0 g/3½ oz brown sugar

00 g/1 lb 2 oz fresh apricots,
stoned and sliced

tsp ground cinnamon

esh clotted cream, to serve

rumble topping

5 g/6 oz wholemeal flour

g/1¾ oz unsalted butter

g/2½ oz brown sugar

g/1¾ oz hazelnuts, toasted
and finely chopped

Preheat the oven to 200°C/400°F/Gas Mark 6. Grease a 1.2-litre/
2-pint ovenproof dish with a little unsalted butter.

Put the unsalted butter and the sugar in a saucepan and
melt together, stirring, over a low heat. Add the apricots and
cinnamon, cover the saucepan and simmer for 5 minutes.

To make the crumble topping, put the flour in a bowl and rub in
the unsalted butter. Stir in the sugar and then the hazelnuts.

Remove the fruit from the heat and arrange in the bottom of
the prepared dish. Sprinkle the crumble topping evenly over the
fruit until it is covered all over. Transfer to the preheated oven
and bake for about 25 minutes until golden.

Serve hot with fresh clotted cream.

DESSERTS

273

APPLE & PLUM CRUMBLE

Preheat the oven to 180°C/350°F/Gas Mark 4.

Mix the apples, plums, apple juice and sugar together in a 23-cm/9-inch round pie dish.

To make the crumble topping, sift the flour into a mixing bowl and rub in the unsalted butter with your fingertips until it resembles coarse breadcrumbs. Stir in the buckwheat and rice flakes, sunflower seeds, sugar and cinnamon, then spoon the topping over the fruit in the dish.

Bake the crumble in the preheated oven for 30–35 minutes, or until the topping is lightly browned and crisp. Serve with cream.

SERVES 4

4 apples, peeled, cored and diced
5 plums, halved, stoned and quartered
4 tbsp fresh apple juice
25 g/1 oz soft light brown sugar
single or double cream, to serve

crumble topping
115 g/4 oz plain flour
75 g/2¾ oz unsalted butter, diced
25 g/1 oz buckwheat flakes
25 g/1 oz rice flakes
25 g/1 oz sunflower seeds
50 g/1¾ oz light brown sugar
¼ tsp ground cinnamon

PEAR & TOFFEE DESSERT

Preheat the oven to 200°C/400°F/Gas Mark 6.

To make the crumble topping, put the flour in a large mixing bowl, then use your fingertips to rub in the unsalted butter until crumbly. Stir in 4 tablespoons of the sugar and the chopped hazelnuts, then cook in the preheated oven for 5–10 minutes until heated through.

To make the toffee, put the golden syrup into a saucepan over a low heat. Add the sugar, unsalted butter, cream and vanilla extract, and bring gently to the boil. Simmer for 3 minutes, stirring constantly, then remove from the heat and set aside.

Put the unsalted butter in a frying pan and melt over a low heat. Meanwhile, peel and roughly chop the pears, then add them to the pan and cook, stirring gently, for 3 minutes. Stir in the toffee and continue to cook, stirring, over a low heat for another 3 minutes.

Transfer the pear-and-toffee mixture to an ovenproof pie dish. Arrange the crumble evenly over the top, then sprinkle over the remaining sugar. Bake in the preheated oven for 25–30 minutes, or until the crumble is golden brown.

Serve hot with vanilla ice cream.

SERVES 4

4 large pears
1 tbsp unsalted butter
vanilla ice cream, to serve

crumble topping

115 g/4 oz self-raising flour
100 g/3½ oz unsalted butter, diced
5 tbsp demerara sugar
2 tbsp finely chopped hazelnuts

toffee

3 tbsp golden syrup
3 tbsp demerara sugar
1 tbsp unsalted butter
2 tbsp single cream
½ tsp vanilla extract

SHERRIED NECTARINE DESSERT

SERVES 4

6 nectarines

25 g/1 oz demerara sugar

2 tbsp sweet sherry

crème fraîche, to serve

crumble topping

185 g/6½ oz plain flour

55 g/2 oz demerara sugar, plus extra for sprinkling

100 g/3½ oz unsalted butter, melted

Preheat the oven to 200°C/400°F/Gas Mark 6.

Using a sharp knife, halve the nectarines, remove and discard the stones, then cut the flesh into fairly thick slices. Put the nectarine slices into an ovenproof pie dish, sprinkle over the sugar and sweet sherry, and cook in the preheated oven for 5–10 minutes until heated through.

To make the crumble topping, put the flour and sugar in a large bowl, then quickly mix in the melted butter until crumbly. Carefully arrange the crumble over the nectarines in an even layer – keep your touch light or the crumble will sink into the filling and go mushy. Scatter a little more sugar over the top, then transfer to the preheated oven and bake for 25–30 minutes, or until the crumble topping is golden brown.

Serve hot with generous spoonfuls of crème fraîche.

GOOSEBERRY & PISTACHIO NUT DESSERT

Preheat the oven to 200°C/400°F/Gas Mark 6.

Top and tail the gooseberries. Put them in an ovenproof pie dish, pour over the honey and cook in the preheated oven for 5–10 minutes until heated through.

Put the caster sugar, orange juice, orange zest and water in a small saucepan and bring to the boil, stirring, over a medium heat. Reduce the heat and simmer for 5 minutes, then remove from the heat and leave to cool.

Meanwhile, to make the crumble topping, put the flour in a bowl, then use your fingertips to rub in the butter until crumbly. Stir in 4 tablespoons of the demerara sugar and the pistachio nuts.

Pour the cooled orange syrup over the gooseberries, then lightly sprinkle over the crumble mixture in an even layer. Do not press the crumble into the syrup or it will become mushy. Sprinkle over the remaining demerara sugar.

Bake in the preheated oven for 25–30 minutes or until the crumble topping is golden brown. Remove from the oven, decorate with strips of orange rind and serve with vanilla ice cream.

SERVES 4

400 g/14 oz gooseberries

1 tbsp honey

85 g/3 oz caster sugar

1 tbsp orange juice

1 tbsp grated orange zest

6 tbsp water

thin strips of orange rind, to decorate

vanilla or orange-flavoured ice cream, to serve

crumble topping

115 g/4 oz self-raising flour

100 g/3½ oz unsalted butter, diced

5 tbsp demerara sugar

50 g/1¾ oz pistachio nuts, finely chopped

PRUNE DESSERT WITH MIXED SPICES

Put the prunes and sultanas in a large bowl, cover with the water and leave to soak overnight or for at least 8 hours.

Preheat the oven to 180°C/350°F/Gas Mark 4.

Drain the fruit, reserving the soaking liquid. Put the fruit in a large saucepan with the sugar and 600 ml/1 pint of the soaking liquid. Bring to the boil, then reduce the heat and simmer for about 10 minutes, or until the fruit has softened.

Meanwhile, to make the crumble topping, put the flour and mixed spice in a bowl, then use your fingertips to rub in the butter until crumbly. Stir in 4 tablespoons of the demerara sugar.

Remove the fruit from the heat, stir in the mixed spice, and the rum, if using, then pour into an ovenproof pie dish. Carefully arrange the crumble over the fruit in an even layer – keep your touch light or the crumble will sink into the filling and go mushy. Scatter the remaining sugar over the top, then transfer to the preheated oven and bake for 25 minutes, or until the crumble topping is golden brown.

Serve hot with crème fraîche.

SERVES 4

225 g/8 oz prunes, chopped

225 g/8 oz sultanas

700 ml/1¼ pints water

3 tbsp demerara sugar

1 tsp mixed spice

1 tbsp dark rum (optional)

crème fraîche, to serve

crumble topping

115 g/4 oz self-raising flour

½ tsp mixed spice

100 g/3½ oz unsalted butter, diced

5 tbsp demerara sugar

FRUIT COBBLER

SERVES 6

600 g/2 lb fresh berries and
  currants, such as blackberries,
  blueberries, raspberries,
  redcurrants and blackcurrants

85–115 g/3–4 oz caster sugar

1 tbsp cornflour

single or double cream, to serve

cobbler topping

200 g/7 oz plain flour

2 tsp baking powder

pinch of salt

55 g/2 oz unsalted butter, diced
  and chilled

2 tbsp caster sugar

175 ml/6 fl oz buttermilk

1 tbsp demerara sugar

Preheat the oven to 200°C/400°F/Gas Mark 6.

Pick over the fruit, mix with the caster sugar and cornflour and
put in a 25-cm/10-inch shallow, ovenproof dish.

To make the cobbler topping, sift the flour, baking powder and
salt into a large bowl. Rub in the unsalted butter until the mixture
resembles breadcrumbs, then stir in the caster sugar. Pour in the
buttermilk and mix to a soft dough.

Drop spoonfuls of the dough on top of the fruit roughly, so that
it doesn't completely cover the fruit. Sprinkle with the demerara
sugar and bake in the preheated oven for 25–30 minutes until the
crust is golden and the fruit is tender.

Remove from the oven and leave to stand for a few minutes
before serving with cream.

DESSERTS

PEACH COBBLER

Preheat the oven to 220°C/425°F/Gas Mark 7.

Put the peaches into a 23-cm/9-inch square ovenproof dish that is also suitable for serving. Add the sugar, lemon juice, cornflour and almond extract and toss together. Bake the peaches in the preheated oven for 20 minutes.

Meanwhile, to make the cobbler topping, sift the flour, all but 2 tablespoons of the sugar, the baking powder and salt into a bowl. Rub in the butter with your fingertips until fine crumbs form. Combine the egg and 5 tablespoons of the milk in a jug and mix into the dry ingredients with a fork until a soft, sticky dough forms. If the dough seems dry, stir in the extra tablespoon of milk.

Reduce the oven temperature to 200°C/400°F/Gas Mark 6. Remove the peaches from the oven and drop spoonfuls of the topping over the surface, without smoothing. Sprinkle with the remaining sugar, return to the oven and bake for a further 15 minutes, or until the topping is golden brown and firm – the topping will spread as it cooks.

Serve hot or at room temperature with ice cream.

6 peaches, peeled and sliced

4 tbsp caster sugar

½ tbsp lemon juice

1½ tsp cornflour

½ tsp almond extract or vanilla extract

vanilla or butter pecan ice cream, to serve

cobbler topping

175 g/6 oz plain flour

115 g/4 oz caster sugar

1½ tsp baking powder

½ tsp salt

85 g/3 oz butter, diced

1 egg

5–6 tbsp milk

STRAWBERRY CREAM COBBLER

Preheat the oven to 200°C/400°F/Gas Mark 6.

Arrange the strawberries evenly in the bottom of an ovenproof dish, then sprinkle over the sugar and cook in the preheated oven for 5–10 minutes until heated through.

Meanwhile, to make the cobbler topping, sift the flour and salt into a large mixing bowl. Rub in the butter until the mixture resembles fine breadcrumbs, then stir in the sugar. Add the beaten egg, then the sultanas and currants, and mix lightly until incorporated. Stir in enough of the milk to make a smooth dough. Transfer to a clean, lightly floured board, knead lightly, then roll out to a thickness of about 1 cm/½ inch. Cut out rounds using a 5-cm/2-inch biscuit cutter. Arrange the dough rounds over the strawberries, then brush the tops with a little milk.

Bake in the preheated oven for 25–30 minutes, or until the cobbler topping has risen and is lightly golden. Serve hot with clotted cream.

SERVES 4

800 g/1 lb 12 oz strawberries, hulled and halved

50 g/1¾ oz caster sugar

clotted cream, to serve

cobbler topping

200 g/7 oz self-raising flour, plus extra for dusting

pinch of salt

3 tbsp butter

2 tbsp caster sugar

1 egg, beaten

25 g/1 oz sultanas

25 g/1 oz currants

about 5 tbsp milk, plus extra for glazing

SPICED MANGO & BLUEBERRY COBBLER

SERVES 4

2 ripe mangoes, stoned and cut into fairly thick slices

250 g/9 oz blueberries

½ tsp nutmeg

1 tbsp lime juice

50 g/1¾ oz caster sugar, or to taste

warm custard, to serve

cobbler topping

200 g/7 oz self-raising flour, plus extra for dusting

pinch of salt

½ tsp cinnamon

3 tbsp unsalted butter

2 tbsp caster sugar

3 tbsp dried blueberries (optional)

1 egg, beaten

about 5 tbsp milk, plus extra for glazing

Preheat the oven to 200°C/400°F/Gas Mark 6.

Put the mango slices and blueberries in the bottom of an ovenproof dish, then sprinkle over the nutmeg, lime juice and caster sugar. Cook in the preheated oven for 5–10 minutes until heated through.

To make the cobbler topping, sift the flour, salt and cinnamon into a large mixing bowl. Rub in the unsalted butter until the mixture resembles fine breadcrumbs, then mix in the sugar, and the dried blueberries, if using. Add the beaten egg, then stir in enough of the milk to make a smooth dough. Transfer to a clean, lightly floured board, knead lightly, then roll out to a thickness of about 1 cm/½ inch. Cut out rounds using a 5-cm/2-inch biscuit cutter. Arrange the dough rounds over the fruit, then brush the tops with a little milk.

Bake in the preheated oven for 25–30 minutes, or until the cobbler topping has risen and is lightly golden.

Serve hot with warm custard.

CHOCOLATE BROWNIES

Preheat the oven to 180°C/350°F/Gas Mark 4. Grease and line a 28 x 18-cm/11 x 7-inch rectangular baking tin.

Put the butter and plain chocolate into a heatproof bowl set over a saucepan of gently simmering water until melted. Remove from the heat. Sift the flour into a large bowl, add the sugar and mix well. Stir the eggs into the chocolate mixture, then beat into the flour mixture. Add the nuts, sultanas and chocolate chips and mix well. Spoon evenly into the prepared tin and level the surface.

Bake in the oven for 30 minutes, or until firm. To check whether the mixture is cooked through, insert a skewer into the centre – it should come out clean. If not, return the tin to the oven for a few minutes. Remove from the oven and leave to cool for 15 minutes. Turn out onto a wire rack to cool completely. To decorate, drizzle the melted white chocolate in fine lines over the top, then cut into squares. Leave to set before serving.

MAKES 15

- 225 g/8 oz butter, diced, plus extra for greasing
- 150 g/5½ oz plain chocolate, chopped
- 225 g/8 oz self-raising flour
- 125 g/4½ oz dark muscovado sugar
- 4 eggs, beaten
- 60 g/2¼ oz blanched hazelnuts, chopped
- 60 g/2¼ oz sultanas
- 100 g/3½ oz plain chocolate chips
- 115 g/4 oz white chocolate, melted, to decorate

CHOCOLATE FUDGE BROWNIES

Preheat the oven to 180°C/350°F/Gas Mark 4. Lightly grease a 20-cm/8-inch square baking tin and line the base.

Beat together the cheese, vanilla extract and 5 teaspoons of caster sugar until smooth, then set aside.

Beat the eggs and remaining caster sugar together until light and fluffy. Place the butter and cocoa powder in a small pan and heat gently, stirring until the butter melts and the mixture combines, then stir it into the egg mixture. Fold in the flour and nuts.

Pour half of the mixture into the tin and smooth the top. Carefully spread the cheese mixture over it, then cover it with the remaining mixture. Bake in the preheated oven for 40–45 minutes. Let cool in the tin.

To make the frosting, melt the butter in the milk in a small pan. Stir in the icing sugar and cocoa powder. Spread the frosting over the brownies and decorate with pecan nuts, if using. Let the frosting set, then cut into squares to serve.

MAKES 16

85 g/3 oz butter,
   plus extra for greasing

200 g/7 oz low-fat soft cheese

½ tsp vanilla extract

225 g/8 oz caster sugar

2 eggs

3 tbsp cocoa powder

100 g/3½ oz self-raising flour,
   sifted

50 g/1¾ oz chopped pecan nuts

fudge frosting

55 g/2 oz butter

1 tbsp milk

75 g/2¾ oz icing sugar

2 tbsp cocoa powder

pecan nuts, to decorate (optional)

DOUBLE CHOCOLATE BROWNIES

MAKES 9 LARGE OR 16 SMALL

115 g/4 oz butter, plus extra
  for greasing

115 g/4 oz plain chocolate, broken
  into pieces

300 g/10½ oz golden caster sugar

pinch of salt

1 tsp vanilla extract

2 large eggs

140 g/5 oz plain flour

2 tbsp cocoa powder

100 g/3½ oz white chocolate
  chips

fudge sauce

55 g/2 oz butter

225 g/8 oz golden caster sugar

150 ml/5 fl oz milk

250 ml/9 fl oz double cream

225 g/8 oz golden syrup

200 g/7 oz plain chocolate,
  broken into pieces

Preheat the oven to 180°C/350°F/Gas Mark 4. Grease and line
the base of an 18-cm/7-inch square baking tin.

Place the butter and chocolate in a small heatproof bowl set
over a saucepan of gently simmering water until melted. Stir until
smooth. Leave to cool slightly. Stir in the sugar, salt and vanilla
extract. Add the eggs, one at a time, and beat until well blended.

Sift the flour and cocoa powder into the mixture and beat until
smooth. Stir in the chocolate chips, then pour the mixture into
the tin. Bake in the preheated oven for 35–40 minutes, or until
the top is evenly coloured and a skewer inserted into the centre
comes out almost clean. Leave to cool slightly while preparing
the sauce.

To make the sauce, place the butter, sugar, milk, cream and
syrup in a small saucepan and heat gently until the sugar has
dissolved. Bring to the boil and stir for 10 minutes, or until the
mixture is caramel-coloured. Remove from the heat and add the
chocolate. Stir until smooth. Cut the brownies into squares and
serve immediately with the sauce.

CAPPUCCINO BROWNIES

Preheat the oven to 180°C/350°F/Gas Mark 4. Grease and line the base of a shallow 28 x 18-cm/11 x 7-inch rectangular baking tin.

Sift the flour, baking powder and cocoa into a bowl and add the butter, caster sugar, eggs and coffee. Beat well, by hand or with an electric whisk, until smooth, then spoon into the prepared tin and smooth the top.

Bake in the oven for 35–40 minutes, or until risen and firm. Leave to cool in the tin for 10 minutes, then turn out onto a wire rack and peel off the lining paper. Leave to cool completely.

To make the frosting, place the chocolate, butter and milk in a bowl set over a saucepan of simmering water and stir until the chocolate has melted. Remove the bowl from the saucepan and sift in the icing sugar. Beat until smooth, then spread over the cake. Dust the top of the cake with sifted cocoa powder, then cut into squares.

MAKES 15

225 g/8 oz butter, softened, plus extra for greasing

225 g/8 oz self-raising flour

1 tsp baking powder

1 tsp cocoa powder, plus extra for dusting

225 g/8 oz golden caster sugar

4 eggs, beaten

3 tbsp instant coffee granules, dissolved in 2 tbsp hot water, cooled

cocoa powder, for dusting

white chocolate frosting

115 g/4 oz white chocolate, broken into pieces

55 g/2 oz butter, softened

3 tbsp milk

175 g/6 oz icing sugar

UPSIDE-DOWN TOFFEE APPLE BROWNIES

Preheat the oven to 180°C/350°F/Gas Mark 4. Grease a 23-cm/ 9-inch square shallow baking tin.

For the topping, place the muscovado sugar and butter in a small pan and heat gently, stirring, until melted. Pour into the prepared tin. Arrange the apple slices over the mixture.

For the brownies, place the butter and sugar in a bowl and beat well until pale and fluffy. Beat in the eggs gradually.

Sift together the flour, baking powder, bicarbonate of soda and mixed spice, and fold into the mixture. Stir in the apples and nuts.

Pour into the prepared tin and bake for 35–40 minutes, until firm and golden. Cool in the tin for 10 minutes, then turn out and cut into squares.

MAKES 9

toffee apple topping
85 g/3 oz light muscovado sugar

55 g/2 oz unsalted butter

1 dessert apple, cored and thinly sliced

brownies
115 g/4 oz unsalted butter, plus extra for greasing

175 g/6 oz light muscovado sugar

2 eggs, beaten

200 g/7 oz plain flour

1 tsp baking powder

½ tsp bicarbonate of soda

1½ tsp ground mixed spice

2 eating apples, peeled and coarsely grated

85 g/3 oz hazelnuts, chopped

CHOCOLATE MARSHMALLOW FINGERS

MAKES 18

350 g/12 oz digestive biscuits

125 g/4½ oz plain chocolate, broken into pieces

225 g/8 oz butter

25 g/1 oz caster sugar

2 tbsp cocoa powder

2 tbsp honey

55 g/2 oz mini marshmallows

100 g/3½ oz white chocolate chips

Put the digestive biscuits in a polythene bag and, using a rolling pin, crush into small pieces.

Put the chocolate, butter, sugar, cocoa and honey in a saucepan and heat gently until melted. Remove from the heat and leave to cool slightly.

Stir the crushed biscuits into the chocolate mixture until well mixed. Add the marshmallows and mix well, then finally stir in the chocolate chips.

Turn the mixture into a 20-cm/8-inch square baking tin and lightly smooth the top. Put in the refrigerator and leave to chill for 2–3 hours, until set. Cut into fingers before serving.

RICH VANILLA ICE CREAM

Pour the whipping cream into a large heavy-based saucepan. Split open the vanilla pod and scrape out the seeds into the cream, then add the whole vanilla pod, too. Bring almost to the boil, then remove from the heat and leave to infuse for 30 minutes.

Put the egg yolks and sugar in a large bowl and whisk together until pale and the mixture leaves a trail when the whisk is lifted. Remove the vanilla pod from the cream, then slowly add the cream to the egg mixture, stirring all the time with a wooden spoon. Strain the mixture into the rinsed-out saucepan or a double boiler and cook over a low heat for 10–15 minutes, stirring all the time, until the mixture thickens enough to coat the back of the spoon. Do not allow the mixture to boil or it will curdle. Remove the custard from the heat and leave to cool for at least 1 hour, stirring from time to time to prevent a skin from forming.

If using an ice cream machine, churn the cold custard in the machine following the manufacturer's instructions. Alternatively, freeze the custard in a freezerproof container, uncovered, for 1–2 hours, or until it begins to set around the edges. Turn the custard into a bowl and stir with a fork or beat in a food processor until smooth. Return to the freezer and freeze.

SERVES 4–6

600 ml/1 pint whipping cream or 300 ml/10 fl oz double cream and 300 ml/10 fl oz single cream

1 vanilla pod

4 large egg yolks

115 g/4 oz caster sugar

CHOCOLATE ICE CREAM

Pour the milk into a large heavy-based saucepan, split open the vanilla pod and scrape out the seeds into the milk and then add the whole vanilla pod, too. Bring almost to the boil then remove from the heat and leave to infuse for 30 minutes. Remove the vanilla pod from the milk. Break the chocolate into the milk and heat gently, stirring all the time, until melted and smooth.

Put the egg yolks and sugar in a large bowl and whisk together until pale and the mixture leaves a trail when the whisk is lifted. Slowly add the chocolate mixture, stirring all the time with a wooden spoon. Strain the mixture into the rinsed-out saucepan or a double boiler and cook over a low heat for 10–15 minutes, stirring all the time, until the mixture thickens enough to coat the back of a wooden spoon. Do not allow the mixture to boil or it will curdle. Remove the custard from the heat and leave to cool for at least 1 hour, stirring from time to time to prevent a skin from forming. Meanwhile, whip the cream until it holds its shape. Keep in the refrigerator until ready to use.

If using an ice cream machine, fold the whipped cream into the cold custard, then churn the mixture in the machine following the manufacturer's instructions. Alternatively, freeze the custard in a freezerproof container, uncovered, for 1–2 hours, or until it begins to set around the edges. Turn the custard into a bowl and stir with a fork or beat in a food processor until smooth. Fold in the whipped cream. Return to the freezer and freeze for a further 2–3 hours, or until firm or required. Cover the container with a lid for storing.

SERVES 4–6

300 ml/10 fl oz milk
1 vanilla pod
100 g/3½ oz plain chocolate
3 egg yolks
85 g/3 oz caster sugar
300 ml/10 fl oz double cream

BUTTERSCOTCH & PECAN ICE CREAM

SERVES 6

300 ml/10 fl oz milk

55 g/2 oz butter

85 g/3 oz soft dark brown sugar

2 eggs

70 g/2½ oz caster sugar

1 tsp vanilla extract

300 ml/10 fl oz whipping cream

100 g/3½ oz pecan nuts, finely chopped

Pour the milk into a saucepan and bring almost to the boil. Remove from the heat. Melt the butter in a heavy-based saucepan, stir in the brown sugar and heat gently until the sugar melts, then boil for 1 minute, or until beginning to caramelize, being careful not to allow the mixture to burn. Remove from the heat and slowly stir in the milk. Return to the heat and heat gently, stirring all the time, until well blended. Remove from the heat and leave to cool slightly. Put the eggs and caster sugar in a large bowl and whisk together until pale. Slowly add the warm milk and vanilla extract, stirring all the time with a wooden spoon.

Strain the mixture into the rinsed-out saucepan or a double boiler and cook over a low heat for 10–15 minutes, stirring all the time, until the mixture thickens enough to coat the back of the wooden spoon. Do not allow the mixture to boil or it will curdle. Remove the custard from the heat and leave to cool for at least 1 hour, stirring from time to time to prevent a skin from forming. Meanwhile, whip the cream until it holds its shape. Keep in the refrigerator until ready to use.

Using an ice cream machine, fold the whipped cream into the cold custard, then churn the mixture in the machine following the manufacturer's instructions. Just before the ice cream freezes, add the chopped pecan nuts. Keep in the freezer until required.

HONEYCOMB ICE CREAM

Grease a baking tray. Put the sugar and syrup in a heavy-based saucepan and heat gently until the sugar melts, then boil for 1–2 minutes, or until beginning to caramelize, being careful not to allow the mixture to burn. Stir in the bicarbonate of soda, then immediately pour the mixture onto the prepared baking tray but do not spread. Leave for about 10 minutes until cold.

When the honeycomb is cold, put in a strong polythene bag and crush into small pieces, using a rolling pin or meat mallet. Whip the cream until it holds its shape, then whisk in the condensed milk.

If using an ice cream machine, churn the mixture in the machine following the manufacturer's instructions. Just before the ice cream freezes, add the honeycomb pieces. Alternatively, freeze the mixture in a freezerproof container, uncovered, for 1–2 hours, or until it begins to set around the edges. Turn the mixture into a bowl and stir with a fork or beat in a food processor until smooth. Fold in the honeycomb pieces. Return to the freezer and freeze for a further 2–3 hours, or until firm or required. Cover the container with a lid for storing.

SERVES 6–8

85 g/3 oz granulated sugar
2 tbsp golden syrup
1 tsp bicarbonate of soda
400 ml/14 fl oz whipping cream
1 can condensed milk

CAPPUCCINO ICE CREAM

Pour the milk and 450 ml/16 fl oz of the cream into a heavy-based saucepan, stir in the coffee and bring almost to the boil. Remove from the heat, leave to infuse for 5 minutes, then strain through a filter paper or a sieve lined with muslin.

Put the egg yolks and sugar in a large bowl and whisk together until pale and creamy. Slowly add the milk mixture, stirring all the time with a wooden spoon. Strain the mixture into the rinsed-out saucepan or a double boiler and cook over a low heat for 10–15 minutes, stirring all the time, until the mixture thickens enough to coat the back of the spoon. Do not allow the mixture to boil or it will curdle. Remove the custard from the heat and leave to cool for at least 1 hour, stirring from time to time to prevent a skin from forming.

If using an ice cream machine, churn the cold custard in the machine following the manufacturer's instructions. Alternatively, freeze the custard in a freezerproof container, uncovered, for 1–2 hours, or until it begins to set around the edges. Turn the custard into a bowl and stir with a fork or beat in a food processor until smooth. Return to the freezer and freeze for a further 2–3 hours, or until firm or required. Cover the container with a lid for storing.

Serve sprinkled with cocoa powder and decorated with chocolate-coated coffee beans.

SERVES 4

150 ml/5 fl oz milk

600 ml/1 pint whipping cream

4 tbsp fresh coffee

3 large egg yolks

115 g/4 oz caster sugar

cocoa powder, for dusting

chocolate-coated coffee beans, to decorate

CRUSHED CHERRY ICE CREAM

SERVES 6

115 g/4 oz caster sugar

150 ml/5 fl oz water

225 g/8 oz fresh cherries, stoned, plus extra whole cherries to decorate

2 tbsp freshly squeezed orange juice

300 ml/10 fl oz double cream

150 ml/5 fl oz single cream

Put the sugar and water in a heavy-based saucepan and heat gently, stirring, until the sugar has dissolved, then bring to the boil and boil for 3 minutes. Reduce the heat, add the cherries and simmer gently for about 10 minutes, or until soft. Leave the mixture to cool for at least 1 hour.

When the cherries are cold, put them in a food processor or blender with the syrup. Add the orange juice and process the cherries until just roughly chopped. Do not blend too much as the cherries should be crushed, not puréed. Pour the double cream and single cream into a large bowl and whip together until the mixture holds its shape. Fold in the crushed cherries.

If using an ice cream machine, churn the mixture in the machine following the manufacturer's instructions. Alternatively, freeze the mixture in a freezerproof container, uncovered, for 1–2 hours, or until it begins to set around the edges. Turn the mixture into a bowl and stir with a fork or beat in a food processor until smooth. Return to the freezer and freeze for a further 2–3 hours, or until firm or required. Cover the container with a lid for storing. Serve decorated with whole cherries.

INDEX